T0124675

THE FUNDAMENTAL FAIR PACT

GOVERNMENT REFORMS 101

Jude Jacques, P.D

authorHOUSE®

AuthorHouse™
1663 Liberty Drive
Bloomington, IN 47403
www.authorhouse.com
Phone: 1-800-839-8640

First published by AuthorHouse   8/22/2011

ISBN: 978-1-4634-5252-0 (sc)
ISBN: 978-1-4634-5251-3 (ebk)

Library of Congress Control Number: 2011915255

Printed in the United States of America

Any people depicted in stock imagery provided by Thinkstock are models,
and such images are being used for illustrative purposes only.
Certain stock imagery © Thinkstock.

This book is printed on acid-free paper.

Special thanks to: Hempstead School Board. Hempstead Public Schools Superintendent, **Special thanks to all of my students at Hempstead High school whom I love very much.** Very special thanks to all Hempstead High School teachers, staff, and faculty. A special thanks to my daughter Jade Elizabeth Jacques and my niece Shelley Maxi.

THIS PROJECT IS DEDICATED TO JESUS THE LORD OF Lords
WHO FOUND ME IN SPITE OF MY SINS AND IMPERFECTION. AMEN.

GOVERNMENT REFORMS 101

Since the earthquake in Haiti and Japan that handicapped both countries I was asked to look at their constitutions and revamp them and to make them more humane and sensitive to nature in general.

"As I was born a citizen of a free Country, I feel that, however feeble the influence my voice can have on public affairs, the right of voting on them makes it my duty to study them; and I am happy, when I reflect upon governments, to find my inquiries always furnish me with new reasons for loving that of my own country".

Doing "***GOOD***" is a matter of looking after the part of yourself which matters most, namely your soul. Therefore, a good and a fair society act fairly and virtuously. On the contrary, a good and a fair society acts fairly and virtuously and its citizens are rarely happy. Nothing can harm a fair state. Much has been written about a just society and some progress has been made; but, much still remains to be done. Progress has been slow because the seeds of success and failure are sown in each person. The basic conflict between good and evil spoken of by religion is about the transition from chaos to intelligent order. The evolution of the universe is about natural selection and survival of the fittest. This is a very stressful process! Intelligence is about order, efficiency, security and reducing stress.

In order for intelligence to win out over individual selfish greed, a learning process is required. As more people see the individual advantage of a Just Society, the more rapidly progress will be made.

The Just Society should provide a level playing field for the game of life. Each individual should be able to achieve at their personal best without restricting their fellow human being's opportunities. The rule of law should replace the law of the jungle. In one word, goodness brings wealth and every other blessing.

A society has to have order. It is like a business or a relationship, if the party in charge is not doing what he is supposed to be doing then all you are going to have is chaos. And when you have chaos or when a society is in disarray, this society is as good as dead.

The great, long-running debate about business's role in society is currently caught between two contrasting, and tired, ideological positions.

On one side of the current debate are those who argue that (to borrow Milton Friedman's phrase) the "business of business is business". This belief is most established in Anglo-Saxon economies. On this view, social issues are peripheral to the challenges of corporate management. The sole legitimate purpose of business is to create shareholder value.

On the other side are the proponents of "Corporate Social Responsibility" (CSR), a rapidly growing, rather fuzzy movement encompassing both companies which claim already to practice CSR and sceptical campaign groups arguing they need to go further in mitigating their social impacts. As other regions of the world—parts of continental and central Europe, for example— move towards the Anglo-Saxon shareholder-value model, debate between these sides has increasingly taken on global significance.

That is a pity. Both perspectives obscure in different ways the significance of social issues to business success. They also caricature unhelpfully the contribution of business to social welfare. It is time for CEOs of big companies to recast this debate and recapture the intellectual and moral high ground from their critics.

Large companies need to build social issues into strategy in a way which reflects their actual business importance. They need to articulate business's social contribution and define its ultimate purpose in a way that has more subtlety than "the business of business is business" worldview and is less defensive than most current CSR approaches. It can help to view the relationship between big business and society in this respect as an implicit "social contract": Rousseau adapted for the corporate world, you might say. This contract has obligations, opportunities and mutual advantage for both sides.

To explain the basis for such an approach, however, it may help first to pinpoint the limitations with the two current ideological poles. Start with the "business of business is business". The issue here is not primarily legal. In many countries, such as Germany, the legal obligation anyway is to stakeholders, and even in America the legal primacy of shareholders is open to very broad interpretation.

The problem with "the business of business" mindset is rather that it can blind management to two important realities. The first is that social issues are not so much tangential to the business of business as fundamental to it. From a defensive point of view, companies that ignore public sentiment make themselves vulnerable to attack. But social pressures can also operate as early indicators of factors core to corporate profitability: for example, the regulations and public-policy environment in which companies must operate; the appetite of consumers for certain goods above others; and the motivation (and willingness to be hired in the first place) of employees.

Companies that treat social issues as either irritating distractions or simply unjustified vehicles for attack on business are turning a blind eye to impending forces that have the potential fundamentally to alter their strategic future. Although the effect of social pressure on these forces may not be immediate, this is not a reason for companies to delay preparing for or tackling them. Even from a strict shareholder-value perspective, most stockmarket value—typically over 80% in American and western European public markets—depends on expectations of companies' cashflow beyond the next three years.

Examples abound of the long-term business impact of social issues. These are growing fast. In the pharmaceuticals sector, a storm of social pressures over the last decade—stemming from issues such as public perceptions of excessive prices charged for HIV drugs in developing countries, for example—are now translating into a general (and sometimes seemingly indiscriminate) toughening in the regulatory environment. In the food and restaurant sector, meanwhile, the long-escalating debate about obesity is now resulting in calls for further controls on the marketing of unhealthy foods. In the case of big financial institutions, concerns over conflicts of interest and mis-selling of products have recently led to changes in core business practices and industry structure. For some big retailers, public and planning resistance to new stores is constraining growth opportunities. And all this is to say nothing of how social and political pressures have reshaped and redefined the tobacco industry, say, or the oil and mining industries over the decades.

In all such cases, billions of dollars of shareholder value have been put at stake as the result of social issues that ultimately feed into fundamental drivers of corporate performance. In many instances, a "business of business is business" outlook has blinded companies to outcomes (or shifts in their implicit "social contract") which often could have been anticipated.

Just as important, these outcomes have posed not just risks to companies, but also have generated value-creation opportunities. In the case of the pharmaceuticals sector, for example, in the growing market for generic (ie, non-patent-protected) drugs; in the case of fast-food restaurants, in providing healthier meals; and in the case of the energy industry, in meeting fast-growing demand (as well as regulatory pressure) for cleaner fuels such as natural gas. Social pressures often indicate the existence of unmet social needs or consumer preferences. Businesses can gain advantage by spotting and supplying these before their competitors.

Paradoxically, the language of shareholder value may hinder companies from maximising shareholder value in this respect. Practised as an unthinking mantra, it can lead managers to focus excessively on improving the short-term performance of their business, neglecting important longer-term opportunities and issues. The latter would include not just societal pressures, but also the trust of customers, investment in innovation and other growth prospects.

The second point that the "business of business is business" outlook obscures for many companies is related to the first: the need to address questions around their ethics and legitimacy. For reasons of integrity and enlightened self-interest, big firms need to tackle such issues, in both words and actions.

It is neither sufficient nor wise to say that it is up to governments to set laws, and for companies simply to operate within these rules. Nor is it enough, even if it is often valid, to point out that many criticisms of businesses are unmerited, or that those throwing the mud ought also to examine their own practices and social responsibility. Irrespective of whether the criticisms are valid or not, their cumulative effect can shape the strategic context for companies. It is imperative for business to seek to lead rather than react to these debates.

Moreover, in some parts of the world, particularly in some poor developing countries, the rule of law as well as provision of basic public services is notable by its absence. This can render the "business of business is business" positively unhelpful as a guide for corporate action. If companies operating in such environments focus too narrowly on ill-defined local laws or shy from broad debates about their alleged behaviour, they are likely to face mounting criticism over their activities, and face a greater risk of becoming embroiled in local political tensions.

Is CSR the answer? If only it were. This is not to criticize the many laudable CSR initiatives by individual companies, or to dispute the obvious need for businesses (as for any other social entity) to be responsible. It is rather to examine the broad prescriptions set for companies by groups and activists involved in CSR. These commonly include "stakeholder dialogue", "social and environmental reports" and corporate policies on ethical issues. This approach is too limited, too defensive and too disconnected from corporate strategy.

The defensive posture of CSR springs from its genesis. Its popularity as a set of tactics among companies was driven in large part by a series of anti-corporate campaigns in the late 1990s. These were given impetus in turn by the anti-globalisation protests around the same time. Since then companies have been drawn to CSR, attracted by nice-sounding, if vague notions such as the "triple bottom line" (the idea that companies can simultaneously serve social and environmental goals as well as profits). They have seen it as a means to avoid NGO and reputational flak, and to mitigate the rougher edges and consequences of capitalism.

This defensiveness starts the argument on the wrong foot, certainly as far as business leaders should be concerned. Big business provides huge and critical contributions to modern society. These are insufficiently articulated, acknowledged or understood. Among these are productivity gains, innovation and research, employment, large-scale investments, human-capital development and organisation. All of these are, and will be, essential for future national and global economic welfare. Big business also provides a vehicle for investment that is likely to be central to the provision of pensions in the ageing OECD. In poorer developing countries, meanwhile, the entry of multinational companies (through foreign direct investment) has often contributed critical capital, technology, skills and other poverty-reducing economic spillovers. It is no coincidence that developing countries place such emphasis on attracting big businesses and the investment it can bring to their economies.

CSR is limited as an agenda for corporate action because it fails to capture the potential importance of social issues for corporate strategy. Admittedly companies undertaking "stakeholder dialogue" with NGOs will be more aware in advance of potential issues. But tracking NGO opinion is only a part of understanding the range of social pressures which ultimately can affect core business drivers such as regulations, consumption patterns and the like.

An obvious next step for companies, having understood the possible evolution of these broad social pressures, is to map long-term options and responses to them. This process clearly needs to be rooted in strategic development. Yet typical CSR initiatives—a new ethical policy here, for example, or a glossy sustainability report there—are often tangential to this. It is perfectly possible for a firm to follow many of the prescriptions of CSR and still to be caught short by seismic shifts in its socially-driven business environment.

One of the compounding problems is that many companies have chosen to root their CSR functions too narrowly within their public- or corporate-affairs departments. Though playing an important tactical role, such departments are often geared towards rebutting criticism, and tend to operate at a distance from strategic decision-making within the company.

In the limitations of both CSR and of the "business of business is business" thinking lie the outlines of a new approach for business (as relevant for Chinese, Indian and German companies as for American and British businesses). Three main strands stand out.

The first is a helpfully simple prescription. Businesses need to introduce explicit processes to make sure that social issues and emerging social forces are discussed at the highest levels as part of overall strategic planning. This means executive managers must educate and engage their boards of directors. It also means they need to develop broad metrics or summaries that usefully describe the relevant issues, in much the same way that most firms analyse customer trends today. The risk that stakeholders—including governments, consumer groups, lawyers and the media—will mobilise around particular issues can be roughly estimated based on the known agendas and interests of these groups. For example, that the obesity debate would rebound before long on the food companies was partly predictable from the growing spending by governments on obesity-related health problems, inevitable media focus on the issue, plus the interest of some lawyers in finding fresh corporate targets for litigation. By the time business seriously engaged with the issue, however, it was in a defensive posture, struggling to catch up with the public debate. In future, companies need to be much better at understanding and anticipating such issues.

The second and third strands both relate to the idea that there is an implicit contract between big business and society, or indeed between whole economic sectors and society—the contract that is the subject of this article. Detractors have often successfully portrayed the contract as a one-way bargain that benefits business at society's expense. Reality is much more complex. The activities undertaken by business have clearly brought social benefits as well as costs. Similarly, however, there are two sides to a contract—and business must acknowledge that in return for the ability to function it is subject to rules and constraints. At times the contract can come under obvious strain. The recent backlash against big business in America can be seen as society seeking to shift the terms of the contract, based on popular perceptions that business has abused its role. Similarly in Germany at present, business is struggling to defend itself against charges that its contract with society is fundamentally unbalanced.

The second strand requires companies not just to understand their individual "contracts", but actively to manage them. To do this they can choose from a range of potential tactics such as: more transparent reporting; shifts in R&D or asset reorganisation to capture expected future opportunities or to shed perceived liabilities; changes in regulatory approach; and, at an industry level, development and deployment of voluntary standards of behaviour.

Some companies and sectors are already experimenting with such approaches—witness General Electric's recent announcement of a doubling of its research spending on environmentally-friendlier technologies.

Nonetheless, there is scope for much more activity, provided it is aligned with corporate strategic goals. Reshaping conduct on an industry-wide and increasingly global basis may be particularly important given that the perceived misdeeds of one company can rebound on its sector as a whole.

An important point is that companies will have quite different tactical responses depending on their circumstances, so off-the-shelf or simply nice-sounding solutions may not always be appropriate. Transparency offers a good example. It is easy, but wrong, to say that there can never be enough of it. What might be good for a pharmaceutical firm trying to restore consumers' trust could be damaging for a hedge-fund manager. And a voluntary code of practice for a retailer naturally would read very differently from that of a copper-mining company.

This leads me to the third strand of a new approach for business leaders. They need to shape the debates on social issues much more consciously. This means establishing ever higher standards of integrity and transparency within their own companies. It also means becoming much more actively involved in external debates and in the media on social issues that shape their business context.

A starting point may be for CEOs to articulate publicly the purpose of business in less dry terms than shareholder value. Shareholder value should continue to be seen as the critical measure of business success. However, it may be more accurate, more motivating—and indeed more beneficial to shareholder value over the long term—to describe business's ultimate purpose as the efficient provision of goods and services that society wants.

This is a hugely valuable, even noble, purpose. It is the fundamental basis of the contract between business and society, and forms the basis of most people's real interactions with business. CEOs could point out that profits should not be seen as an end in themselves, but rather as a signal from society that their company is succeeding in its mission of providing something people want—and doing it in a way that uses resources efficiently relative to other possible uses. From this perspective, shareholder-value creation or profits are the measure, and the reward, of success in delivering to society the more fundamental business purpose. The measures and rewards reflect the predominant values of the relevant society.

By moving away from a rigid linguistic focus on shareholder value, big business can also make clear to a broad audience that it understands the trade-offs that are inherent in its social contract. The debate between business and society is essentially one over the management of, and agreement over, those trade-offs.

What might this mean specifically? There is no shortage of big social issues today that directly affect many big businesses and that require new debate. These include: ensuring aid and trade regimes successfully promote the development of Africa and other poor regions (the economic lift-off of such regions would present a major potential boon to global markets as well as international security); promoting a more sophisticated and sensitive approach from both companies and governments to balancing the societal risks and rewards from new technologies; spearheading dialogue on the health-care and pension challenges in many developed countries; and supporting efforts to resolve regional conflicts.

Obviously the relevant issue needs to be matched to the specific business. Some companies and business organisations have taken strong public stances on these and similar issues. But in general high-level, concerted corporate activism is more notable by its absence.

Business leaders should not fear their greater advocacy of the contract between business and society. Public receptiveness to active business leadership on issues such as these may be a lot better than some might be inclined to think. Despite the poor image and bad press of big business in recent times, polls suggest that people retain a belief in the ability of business to provide a positive contribution to society.

More than two centuries ago, Rousseau's social contract helped to seed the idea among political leaders that they must serve the public good, lest their own legitimacy be threatened. The CEOs of today's big corporations should take the opportunity to restate and reinforce their own social contracts in order to help secure, for the long term, the invested billions of their shareholders.

What is suitable for a fair and just country is a mixed government, where the people assemble by sections rather than as a whole, and where those who are entrusted with power are changed at frequent intervals. This form of government will produce two great advantages. First, by confining the work of administration to a small number only, it will permit the choice of enlightened men. Secondly, by requiring the cooperation of all members of the state in the exercise of the supreme authority, it will place all on a plane of perfect equality.

The fundamental law of the country must be really equality. Everything must be related to it, including even authority, which established only to defend it. All should be equal by right of birth; the state should grant no distinctions except to merit, to virtue, and to services done for the nation.

New System of government:

RETIREES
EX-PRESIDENT
MINISTERS
DOCTORS
TEACHERS AND ADMINISTRATORS
COMMERCANTS

The above people are the supreme councils and the engine of the government, because they are trusted and elected by the people to select the followings:
MINISTER OF WOMEN AND CHILDREN
MINISTER OF EDUCATION
MINISTER OF FINANCE
MINISTER OF HEALTH
MINISTER OF AGRICULTURE
MINISTER OF PUBLIC RELATIONS AND ENVIRONMENT
MINISTER OF HOMELAND SECURITY
MINISTER OF NATURAL RESOURCES AND ROADS AND HIGHWAYS
MINISTER OF THE ARMY
MINISTER OF JUSTICE
MINISTER OF TECHNOLOGY AND GREEN ENVIRONMENT
MINISTER OF THE ELDERLY

N.B A government does not have to follow this pattern exactly, but it has to be close in order to be a fair, humane, just government.

The term minister should be changed to Facilitator. A facilitator is someone who helps a group of people understand their common objectives and assists them to plan to achieve them without taking a particular position in the discussion.

Facilitators are Members of Parliament who are given additional responsibility by the Prime Facilitator. The Prime Facilitator chooses experienced and knowledgeable parliamentarians from the same party or party coalition. All the facilitators should work together for the betterment of the government. Senior government facilitators meet each week in Cabinet to consider ideas for new laws and solutions to solve current problems.

Each facilitator is in charge of a department such as the Department of Defense Ministers work with their department and with other community organizations, and professional associations to prepare new laws and change old laws which need updating or improving. When a minister introduces a bill for a new law into the Parliament, he or she must explain to the Parliament why the law is necessary and how it will solve a particular problem. As soon as the bill becomes law, the minister and the department are responsible for implementing it throughout Australia.

All ministers must be able to stand up in Parliament each day at 2pm during Question Time and answer questions from other members and senators about their departments and how the government is running Australia. Ministers in the government are responsible to the Parliament, and any members and senators can examine, scrutinize and criticize the work of the government through the work of each facilitator.

Shadow facilitators are members who belong to the opposition party. Although they have no power, they have a responsibility to scrutinize the work of the government and of individual facilitator.

All of his or her parliamentary party as shadow facilitators who, like government ministers, concentrate on the work of particular departments such as Defense. Senior shadow facilitators form a shadow cabinet which meets regularly and discusses opposition policy on current issues. Shadow facilitators also explain to the Parliament what the opposition would do about specific problems if the opposition were the government.

If there is a change of government after an election the shadow facilitators are all expected to become facilitators.

> The twelve sub-councils or facilitators report directly to the above council members. If a member of the council becomes corrupt. He or She will be terminated, jailed and be replaced immediately. It is a big risk for a council to take because such action might jeopardize the family last name. A corrupted council should never be part or elected to any organizations again. His name shall become a nightmare for the society which he lives in.

Along with the fact you stated Trace, if we do not present proposal(s) for reparations on President Obama's Desk within the next 2 - 3 years, we can forgettaboutit!!!

As far as the Congressional Reform Act of 2011 below, I boldly state that all non-Black members of Congress should adhere to the information below (or just Republicans). Reparations package should also demand free college education for Black children (with certain realistic criteria), Youth Depots built throughout our communities (instead of prisons), free healthcare, and a list of other holistic opportunistic services that we can collectively benefit from. It is better to provide ways to teach each other, and future generations, how to fish, than to just give out fish.

Part of the reason things are happening the way they are is because people do not vote as they should. When your voices is heard loud and clear that is when change occurs. How fast can this get around the country? The 26th amendment (granting the right to vote for 18 year-olds) took only 3 months & 8 days to be ratified! Why? Simple! The people demanded it. That is in 1971 before computers, before e-mail, before cell phones, etc. Of the 27 amendments to the Constitution, seven (7) took 1 year or less to become the law of the land...all because of public pressure.

I'm asking each addressee to forward this email to a minimum of twenty people on their address list; in turn ask each of those to do likewise.

In three days, most people in The United States of America will have the message. This is one idea that really should be passed around.

Congressional Reform Act of 2011
1. Term Limits: 12 years only, one of the possible options below..
A. Two Six-year Senate terms
B. Six Two-year House terms
C. One Six-year Senate terms and three Two-Year House terms
2. No Tenure / No Pension.
A Congressman collects a salary while in office and receives no pay when they are out of office.
3. Congress (past, present & future) participates in Social Security.
All funds in the Congressional retirement fund move to the Social Security system immediately. All future funds flow into the Social Security system, and Congress participates with the American people.
4. Congress can purchase their own retirement plan, just as all Americans do.
5. Congress will no longer vote themselves a pay raise. Congressional pay will rise by the lower of CPI or 3%.
6. Congress loses their current health care system and participates in the same health care system as the American people.
7. Congress must equally abide by all laws they impose on the American people.
8. All contracts with past and present Congressmen are void effective 1/1/12.

The American people did not make this contract with Congressmen. Congressmen made all these contracts for themselves.

Serving in Congress is an honor, not a career. The Founding Fathers envisioned citizen legislators, so ours should serve their term(s), then go home and back to work.

In order for a country to produce productive citizens, people have to be fully held accountable for their actions, non-actions and behaviors. Any society that rewards bad behavior with a little slap on the wrist, a lot of its citizens tend to repeat the same behavior over and over again. However, if people know that the consequences for their actions will be grave and embarrassing they tend to stay away from unfruitful behavior.

Behavior refers to the actions or reactions of an object or organism, usually in relation to the environment. Behavior can be conscious or subconscious, overt or covert, and or the first thing it takes for this system of government to work is to reeducate the people especially, the proletariat. The class of wage earners, esp. those who earn their living by manual labor or who are dependent for support on daily or casual employment; the working class.

Reeducating means that the system that's in place or the status-quo needs to shut down. Rep. Michele Bachmann, who has levied the most bizarre and outlandished critiques against President Obama since before he came into office, did not disappoint this weekend. Appearing on Minnesota radio station KTLK-AM, the Republican congresswoman expressed her concern that White House was trying to put in place "re-education camps for young people, where young people have to go and get trained in a philosophy that the government puts forward." Furthering the Obama-as-autocrat theme, Bachmann said the youngsters would "then they have to go to work in some of these politically correct forums."

Just for the record I am not talking about reorganization. The old system needs to be dismantled totally, so we can start producing citizens who really care for and about their countries I asked a few of my students what makes a good student. This is what they said "

ANGEL

To be a good citizen, you need to be involved in your community. Also, a good citizen respects other people's property. Finally, to be a good citizen, you need to know what's happening in your community. If you're a good citizen, the community will be a better place to live.

It's important to know what's happening in your community. At least that's what a good citizen would do. A good citizen would know what's happening whether it's good or bad. If everyone were a bad citizen, there would be much confusion. Also, if everyone were a good citizen there would be no confusion. That is why you should be a good citizen. You don't want confusion in your community. That's why it's important to be a good citizen.

A good citizen is involved in their community. They could make the town a better place by cleaning it up. Also, a good citizen could also organize the town events. If everyone were a good citizen, the town would be a much better place to live. That is why it's important to be a good citizen. In addition, if everyone were a bad citizen, the town wouldn't be good place to live. It wouldn't be a good thing to live in a bad community. So, you have to be a good citizen.

A good citizen respects other people's property. So, you need to be a good citizen. If you weren't a good citizen, the communities would be a bad place to live. That's why you need to be a good citizen. Furthermore, if everyone were a good citizen, nothing would ever be stolen. That is also why you should be a good citizen. If there were no thieves, how could you're property be stolen? Those are some reasons you should be a good citizen.

Still want to know how to be a good citizen? Well, you just read the answer to it in those three paragraphs! The time has come for you to know the answer to the other question as well. To be a good citizen, you need to do these three things: First, be involved in your community. Second, you need to respect other people's property. Finally, you need to know what's happening in your community. That is what it takes to be a good citizen.

ALANA

Can an eleven-year-old, like me, be a good citizen? Of course they can! They can get involved with community issues and debate about wars. All kids can also follow the laws. Finally, I think everyone should be nice to other people. This essay will only take a few minutes of your time.

One way to be a good citizen is to get involved with wars and community issues. Maybe you're thinking, "Who cares?" right now just like thousands of others. I can only tell you a few of the people who do care. The troops in Iraq who risk their lives to protect us are a good example of this. Others are the people whose lives are affected by the wars. Also, the government cares because it helps a lot of people. Here are some ways you can get involved. You can listen to news or radio broadcasts for information. People can also read newspaper articles. The main way to get involved is to have a part in the issue.

Another way to be a good citizen is to obey the law. If you do not follow the law, there will always be consequences. Even if you escape, you will have to go into hiding. Here are only three laws, but they are some you should always follow. You should never commit murder because you are killing innocent people. You should never steal either, because it is someone's property you would be taking.

Last of all, you shouldn't go over the speed limit. The speed limit is a safety measure, and without it, it becomes easier to crash and possibly kill people.

And lastly, you should always be nice to people. Because you wouldn't want to be treated unkindly, you shouldn't treat others that way either. Here are three ways you can be nice to people: One way is to help people that need help. That will make their lives a lot easier. Another way is to share with them so they can enjoy what you have. It will make them happier also. And the last reason is to be cheerful to everyone around you, so they will be happy too.

I have only listed three ways kids and adults alike can be good citizens; getting involved by debating in wars or government issues, following the law, and being kind to people. Now that you have read this essay, I hope you will apply these things to your life so you can become a good citizen too.

JOHN

Being a good citizen is a good thing to do. To be a good citizen you can help people. You can stay involved with the city, and you can do the right stuff. Kids now can also be a good citizen. I am going to talk about those things in my report.

Staying involved is one thing you could do to be a better citizen. If you stay involved you can know what's going on in the world. For example, you could stay involved in the world by watching the news and reading the news paper. By staying involved you will also know about the people in your community. You could learn about whom you should be friends with. You will know what your neighbors are like and what your neighborhood is like as well. That way you could make friends with the right people. That's one thing you could do to be a better citizen.

Helping others is another way to be a good citizen. If you help others you will be doing the right thing. For example, if someone gets hurt you should help them. You would also be helping someone that needed help. So when you need help they will help you. When you help people they think of you as a good citizen. Helping people will make you a good citizen, and it also makes you feel better to help people. In my opinion those are some reasons why it is good to help others and some good examples on how to become a better citizen.

If you do the right thing you will be a good member of the community and a good citizen. By doing something to help clean up around the community it would be a way to do something right. Participating in fundraisers is also a good way to help around the community. Supporting local sports will also help make you be a good member of your community. Volunteering in schools is a good way to help your community too. When you make good choices people will remember you for it. People will know that you are a good citizen. Being a good citizen is important to the success of a good community.

In my opinion these are all good ways in which a person could be a good citizen and a member of the community. Helping others is important to make your community a better place. By staying involved and participating in community activities, fundraiser and volunteering one can show how they care about there community. I hope more people will get involved in our community. I plan to do my part in being a good citizen.

Sophia

Being a good citizen is learning and developing good life skills. The next idea of becoming a good citizen is being organized. The final idea I will explore in this paper is staying involved with your community. I believe becoming a better citizen is important because you can create a better relationship with others.

The first piece of being a good citizen is having good life skills, like being responsible. Being responsible means keeping track of your belongings at all times. For example, when you go on a sleepover don't forget your socks or toothbrush. Another part is doing your chores or jobs on time. If your job is taking the trash out on Tuesday and you forget, you're stuck with a whole bunch of trash. Speaking of time, one more part of being responsible is being in the right place at the right time, like not being late for school, appointments, and sport practices. If you are late to school too many times you will get after school detention, and you have to make up missed work. Being late for practice may cause you to run extra laps and you would be letting the coach and your team down. Being responsible is the first strategy to becoming a better citizen.

The next part of being a better citizen is being organized. It is important for students to keep their locker in tack, so they don't lose any important papers. If you lose assignments you lose points and get bad grades. If you get bad grades you might get held back. The solution to this is putting your worksheet into your binder behind the right tab. Along with keeping your binder organized make sure your text books and dear book are where you can get to them easily. Getting to your text books is important because you only have five minutes in-between classes. So as you see being organized is important part of being a good citizen.

The final part of being a good citizen is being involved with your community. Volunteering to coach a sport team is good community service. This is important to the kids, so more kids can play they are always looking for good coaches. Volunteering at church is a great idea for serving your community. For example I help with Awana in game time along with George. Another way you can volunteer is to organize a canned food drive in your community. We need canned food drives so we can help families who are less fortunate than others. The last way you can stay involved, with your children and talk about what they should stay away from. For example drugs, alcohol, and people who are bad influences. This will help to make them better citizens.

Those are just a few thought of what I believe makes a good citizen. That is why we have kind and helpful Americans today. If we all try to be better citizens we will form a better tomorrow.

Golo

Being a good citizen is important. I think that citizenship is unexciting but it is important. What this paper is about is voting. It is also about how it's important to be educated about the war and follow laws. That is what this paper is about.

To make a good citizen is voting. It is important to vote because if you don't vote you have no right to complain. Sometimes it is good to complain because you can make the United States better. Voting is choosing who you want to be president. Also, it is important to vote because when you vote you are participating in being a U.S. citizen. Being a good U.S. citizen means to follow laws. Also, being a good U.S. citizen means to say the Pledge of Allegiance very day and singing the national anthem before a baseball game. It is important to vote.

Another way to be a good U.S. citizen is being educated about the war. Being educated about the war means many different things. You need to know what is going on in the war. There are many ways you can find out about the war, like reading newspapers and watching the news. You'll need to know where the war is going on. Finding out where it's going on is just a matter of looking on a map. Knowing who's involved in the war is very important. You can also find this out on the news or in the newspaper.

Another thing that makes a good citizen is obeying the law. Don't vandalize another people's property. That means don't graffiti and destroy other people's stuff. Do not kill people. You need to follow the speed limit to be a good citizen. If you don't follow the speed limit you could hurt yourself and others. There are consequences for these things. You could go to prison or get a ticket.

It is good to be a good citizen. You have read all about being a good citizen. Voting is part of being a good citizen. It is important to be educated about the war and follow the laws. Now you know what it means to be a good citizen, so go be one.

FELIX

Hello I am Grant B. I am going to tell you about things that I can do to be a good citizen. It could be something as simple as recycling a used soda can, or putting yard debre in a yard recyclables bin.

Being a good citizen is fun in many ways. You can have fun while still being a good citizen. Picking up trash in the park can be fun if you do it with friends. Educating your peers about drugs and alcohol is a good contribution. Also you can help pass out and advertise merchandise to help raise money for a charity. Or help educate your community about false advertisement. You could also tell your community why gas prices are so high. My beliefs of why the gas prices are so high are that because of the war and our government needs money to support our troops. Additionally the oil companies are taking advantage of the situation.

You can be a good citizen while still being a good friend. Like when a friend needs help with homework. And when a teacher needs help with the classroom. And you could also be a good citizen by helping your neighborhood. Being a good citizen is to inform your neighborhood of hazards.

If you want to be a good citizen you can educate your community about Iraq. The war in Iraq is often misunderstood. Some people can think that the war is pointless. I believe that if we pull out our troops that they will just fire up their weapons plants and bomb us in the near future.

These are some of the many things you can do to help improve your neighborhood. Don't you think it's time you took on some responsibility?

GOMEZ

What does it mean to be a good citizen? Being a good citizen could mean a bunch of things, like helping others, being involved in the community, or learning about the government. These are all great ways to be involved in the community. There are other ways but this essay is going to talk about those three main things.

We need to be involved in the community. Some ways we can do that is by going to city council meetings. If the city is doing something or not doing something, don't just sit and watch it happen. Go and tell them what you think. Another way is to volunteer to do repairs on stuff or help plant grass. You could also arrange a clean up when you go around the town and pick up litter. These would help by making the land cleaner, making it look nicer and being able to do something about it.

We also need to learn about the government. We need to know how the government works. It's important because if we don't think something is right we can vote against it. Or if we don't know how it works and we think something is wrong, then we can learn how it works and understand if it is right. Also we need to vote. Voting is our patriotic duty and we need to honor it. It's important to vote because at least we have a say in it. Some countries have dictators that take a gun and hold it to somebody's head and say "I'm going to be president got it." Last tell others to vote. It's not only your duty it's theirs too.

Last it's important to help others. Like if someone gets hurt give them a bandage or medical attention maybe even call 911. If the accident's bad enough you might save a life. Also if someone is being bullied stop the bully. It might start as teasing but could get a lot worse. You could really help someone. Last if someone is carrying something heavy and drops it help them pick it up. It will make you feel good and you'll get a good reputation.

In conclusion that's what I think being a good citizen means: Helping others, being involved in the community. And learning about the government all great was to be a good citizen.

FRANCISCO

There are many ways to be a good citizen and I feel that kids our age can be a part of it Being involved with the society is one way to be a good citizen. Joining a club or service could be another way. Or maybe you could just be civil and benignant. These are all good ways to becoming a good citizen. As you continue to read you will find the many benefits of these actions and why you might want to be a part of it.

When you are involved with the community you are being a good citizen. How can you be involved with the community? Well, you could start by reading your daily newspaper for reports of anything near your community, so you can stay safe. For example…if there was a burglary nearby, you would know to be extra sure you locked all your doors and windows. Another way is to talk to your neighbors about things going on in their lives, so you could support them when they are going through tough times or congratulate them when they have achieved something. One more thing I can think of is set up meetings with your neighbors and talk about things that need fixing in your area. Such as, if there was a hole in your road you could all chip in some money to get it fixed. It would be a lot cheaper and you would improve your area, while you would be well known and respected.

Another way to be a good citizen is by joining a club or service. In your club you could pick up trash around town to make your town a cleaner and nicer place to be in. Or, you could collect items to help people in need, such as orphanages, homeless people, or maybe some hurricane or tornado relief. You could also set rules down in your area, to make your area safer. Joining a club is a great way to help out your community and others in need. Join a club and be a part of these acts.

Being civil and benignant is another good way of becoming a good citizen. You can do that by using good language because that is respectful. Another thing you can do is help people who are in need of help. If you see someone's bag fall on the ground and spill…help pick it up. They will see you as a good person and you will be respected for your polite and kind actions. One other way is to respect people's property. Don't walk into someone's flowerbed or lawn. As well as doing graffiti on their possessions. Something like that would be disrespectful. By not doing and doing these things you are being a good citizen.

Kids our age can do all of these things. They can be involved with the society. As well as join a club and help out around their community or even the world. Being civil and benignant isn't so hard either. If you try to become apart of one of these acts, you will be so glad you did. So, become a good citizen and you'll never regret it!

JOSE

I think a good citizen has three main guidelines. First, a good citizen is polite. Second, a good citizen looks out for others. Third, a good citizen follows the law. I think a good citizen is polite, looks out for others and follows the law.

A good citizen is polite. They don't damage property, signs, or other people's houses. Those would not be good neighborly things to do. After having lunch they throw their trash in the garbage. People do this because parks covered in litter aren't good places for kids to play. Good citizens don't do stuff to annoy their neighbors. Neighbors don't do this, because that might make the other neighbor's life miserable and then they could be annoying back which in turn could make life miserable for both neighbors. Good citizens don't damage property, litter, or be bad neighbors.

A good citizen looks out for others. If someone got drunk at a party, a good citizen would let them stay the night or drive them home. They would do this because a drunk driver can be a danger on the road. After leaving home if a good citizen sees someone rob a store they report it. Then others could be on their guard. While coming from work if a good citizen sees people selling drugs he would report it. He would do this because drugs are deadly and addictive, and in order to buy more innocent people could be hurt. Good citizens help neighbors, report robberies, and report drug dealings.

A good citizen follows the law. If while walking his dog, a good citizen sees something he wants, he wouldn't steal it. People don't do this because it would cost the shop owner money to replace it. While driving, a good citizen follows the speed limit. They do this because if while speeding they go around a sharp corner they could roll their car or hurt someone. When mad, good citizens would not harm anyone. Because they might go to jail and the person could go to the hospital. Good citizens don't steal, speed, or harm others.

From my sixth grade point of view, good citizens do three things. Number one, they're polite. Number two, they look out for others. Number three, they follow the law. Good citizens are polite, look out for others, and follow the law.

JUANITA

There are so many ways you can become a good citizen. Being a good citizen is a good thing. If you are a good citizen sometimes you will get awarded. You should also follow the laws. If you are following the laws you are doing a good thing. Another thing you should do is always beware of the environments. The last thing you should do is be nice to others and they'll do the same.

First, always beware the environments. You need to learn how to keep the world clean. One way to keep the world clean is to pick up all the garbage. Another way to keep the world clean is to always recycle. If you donŌt recycle animals will die. there would be more pollution if you did not recycle. Pollution also kills animals. So that is one thing you can do to be a good citizen.

Next, you should always be nice to others. If you were nice to others they would do the same. Do not use bad language. If you use bad language at some one they'll do it back. You should also help your community. You should help your community by cleaning up. If you cleaned up you would be doing something good. You would also be making the world a better place.

One other thing you need to do to be a good citizen is to always follow the laws. One thing you can do is not litter. Another thing you can do is respect others. If you don't they would not want to be your friend any more. That is what you can do to be a good citizen.

You should be a good citizen and do these thing. If you didn't you would be a criminal. In conclusion these are all the things you can do to be a good citizen. These are most of the things you can do to help.

SERGIO

What is a good citizen? This is a question that is not easily answered but kids can still be good citizens. Getting involved in your in your community is one thing kids can do. A little but, helpful thing is volunteering. Being polite is also another thing that makes a good citizen. Being a good citizen is always a very good thing.

One thing that makes a good citizen is, getting involved in your community. One reason of doing that is so you know what you can do to help your community. Like if there is a problem in your community, you may be able to find a solution. You also may miss a great opportunity. Another thing is so you know what is going on in your community. Personally I like to know what is going on in my community. Something else is volunteering, like volunteering to pick up trash at the park so people will have a nice place to play. Another simple thing is reading the newspaper.

Something else that makes a good citizen is volunteering. The simple things of volunteering can make you a good citizen. Volunteering is really simple but still really helpful in many ways. Cleaning up trash may not seem like a lot of help but, it still makes you a good citizen. Painting and fixing up old broken down stuff makes your community a more beautiful place to live in. Helping elders does not affect everyone but it is still something kids can do to be a good citizen. Another thing is to raise money for the homeless. One kid or one person doesn‚Äôt seem like a lot of help but one piece of food, clothing or even a letter means the whole world to one unfortunate person.

The last thing is being polite. It doesn't seem like a lot to be a good citizen or more importantly a good friend. Being nice or polite is an easy way for kids to be a good citizen. It will make your community a better place to live in. In a group effort you will most definitely see you will get stuff done faster and more efficiently. You will most definitely see you will get more respect. A good attitude can make you a good citizen. You will also make your community a happier and brighter place to live in.

Being a good citizen is a lot of work but still something kids should get involved in. Getting involved in your community is one thing. Another thing is volunteering. The last thing is being polite. All of these things and more are things kids can do to be a good citizen.

MAX

There are three big parts to being a good citizen. One of these is being responsible. The second is not committing crimes. The third is knowing what's going on in the world around you and educating others about it as well. These are three major parts to being a good citizen.

Responsibility means taking the consequences for your own actions. Being a good citizen means getting involved in your community. That means volunteering in events like baseball or soccer, but they don't have to be sports. They can be events like parades, festivals or a litter patrol. Voting is another big thing. Voting is very important to your community because you help make decisions. It is also important because you know how to help your community and make a difference. Responsible citizens don't litter, riot or hut other people because of something that they did. A basic form of being responsible is listening to your parents and doing your fair share of work without complaining. Being conscience of other people around you make you a good citizen.

Another way to be a good citizen is to not commit crimes. Drugs are a crime you hear about often. Doing drugs puts innocent people at risk of being killed. It is a quick and easy way to end up in jail. Probably the biggest thing you can do in being responsible is not drinking and driving because you can kill someone. Instead, be responsible by taking a cab or having a designated driver that didn't drink. Murder is a very bad thing. It is not responsible and will put you in jail, or worse. You don't have to be a person's friend but you should not kill them over something. It is not good citizenship commit crimes because it puts innocent people at risk and it puts yourself at risk.

To be a good citizen you should learn and understand what is going on in the world around you. That means you should read the newspaper. The newspaper has a lot of information in it. All the current events are in the newspaper including problems in the government and other issues in the world. You can also get information about storms or other things that might concern you. The television news is the second best way to get information, but you don't always get the right information. It is a lot easier then reading the newspaper. If you talk to others, you can get more information that you have missed. Using this you can educate yourself and other people about the world around you.

I think that all people can be good citizens, but you have to try or it is not possible. Whether it is obeying the law, volunteering, or educating, it is all good citizenship. There are more things that you can do, but it is up to you, no one can choose it for you.

JONATHAN

My feeligs about being a good citizen is that we could all be good in life if we just try. Part of being a good citizenis to be a good friend.One thing to be a good citizen is to be fair. Another is tobe nice to one another.Also not saying bad words.This is how to be a good citizen.

One thing that people could do to be a good citizen is to be nice to people even if you dont like them.If you dont,then other people wont be nice to you.Also if you be nice to people then they willgive you nice things and people wontb be mean to you.People have to be a good citizen because you can bea good helper if anybody needs helpbecause when you need heip on a sertan thing at school you could go to that person that you helped to get the answer.

Being nice to people is a good thing because if your not, then nowone will like you.Another good thing about being nice is to be nice to them even if ther not nice to you.Sometimes its good to be nice because then they wont tell anybody something thats not true about you. This is why it is good to be nice to people.

One thing people could do to be a good citzen is to not say bad words.Sometimes when you say some thing bad or say a bad word you will get intruble.When people say bad words they wont be able to go any wher fun because you got intruble.A second thing if you say bad words than you wont be able to hang out with friends any where.Saying bad words is a bad thing because then people will think that your a bad kid.Peple dont say bad words because you can go places,hang out,and all that fun stuff if you dont say bad words.Another thing not to say bad words is that some people might make fun of you.These are some things why kids shouldnt say bad words.

Also another thing people could do to be a good citizen is to be fair.One thing people should be fair because if yo dont than they might not like you very much because make them feel left out.A second thing that you should be fairis that you can be fair to them even if you dont like them. Sometimes when you dont be fair to other people they wont be fair to you.People wont lown you things or give you nice stuff if your not fair.A third thing that people should be fair because if you dont than people will think that your a mean person and make them feel like they dont belong.Even if you dont like them you still can be fair.These are some ways for kids to know how to be fair in their life.

Being fair not saying bad words and being nice to people are some things that everybody should do all these are good things because everyone will like you like not saying bad words especially these are what you should do to be a good citizen this is what kids should do in their life.

Also another thing people could do to be a good citizen is to be fair one thing people should be fair because if you don't than they might not like you very much because make them feel left out.A second thing that you should be fairis that you can be fair to them even if you dont like them. Sometimes when you dont be fair to other people they wont be fair to you. People wont lown you things or give you nice stuff if your not fair.A third thing that people should be fair because if you don't than people will think that your a mean person and make them feel like they dont belong.Even if you dont like them you still can be fair.These are some ways for kids to know how to be fair in their life.

Being fair,not saying bad words,and being nice to people are some things that evrybody should do.All these are good things because everyone will like you,like not saying bad words expecaily.These are what you should do to be a good citizen.This is what kids should do in their life.

WEB

Do you want to be a good citizen here's a good example! You can support your troops buy writing to them! Also earn money for the fire fighter . I'm only 11 and this is what I would do. Help people in need . You should stand up and be there for others. Clean up your room for your mom and dad . Finely you should clean up around you!

To be a good citizen be proud of what you do! You can raise money for the fire fighters and so they can have money for parts on the truck. Also for them self's Like clothes if they burned in fire or there cloths are to small so they can buy new ones! How to raise money is easy you could do a lemonade stand or you could do a garage sale You can buy stuffed animals for if a little boy or girls house burned down .There stuffed animals had burned. To give a stuffed animal or a toy to the fire fighters or the police . So get involved and do the boy/girl needs you they will love the stuffed animal or toy. You will feel like you made a difference.

Also if you want to help , think about the army . Help them and if you know someone there give candy or food and coffee toy and they love letters . Send them a letter. They love them even if you don't know them. Still all I am saying is write a letter to them. They love them. Tell them a joke .Write to them you love them just write the letter! Hey all i am saying is get involved. Don't be a sour puss!

Finally, to be proud good citizen you should be active in school! That means you should be in a lot of activities like prevention club and others .It will be a lot of fun and you will be smarter. Do big projects to show other people would you can do. You will be a lot friendlier with others. So get in school activities and go for it.

So all I'm saying is to be proud of what you do so send money to fire fighters and police! Write to the army and be active in school ! ta ta for now!

NOEL

What makes good citizenship? Good citizenship is being involved. Being involved can be difficult. You need to keep up with the news. It is important because if we were going to war you'd want to know. Also it is important to be nice to people.

Sometimes being involved can cause problems. But if you work hard at it you can accomplish many things. It is important to be involved because you would know what's going on around you. Next you would know how to react. There are three main reasons why it is important to be involved. Just like there is a war and many people are reacting differently. Another way that people are reacting is that people are tuning into the radio stations and the tv news. All of these are ways to stay involved.

It is also important to keep up with your country. One way to do that is to read the paper and to watch the news. By doing this you will have an idea of what's going on. If we were to go to war you wouldn't know when or why. It is important to always vote for whom you support. Just simple things like that can keep you involved.

It is also important to be nice. The reason it is important is because you would want to be treated with respect. Another is people wouldn't be nice to you. Another reason is that people have a reputation. Or the people of the community might know something that person doesn't want anybody else to know. If you were not nice people would treat you the same. You wouldn't want to be treated badly. So put yourself in their shoes. All of these are good reasons to be nice.

Being a good citizen can mean many things. For one you could listen to the radio. Secondly, you could try to know what's going on. You should always be nice. It is very important to keep up with the country. To be a good citizen you also need to help the people who need it the most.

Marlo

I'm a good citizen because I've done a lot of help fall things. I've donated toys to goodwill for kids. I've done find raisers, when i do these things it helps a lot of kids out. I study hard so i can do well in school and jobs when I'm older. Also when I or other people donate things to soldiers it makes soldiers happy. There are simple ways to make a difference and these are just some of the ways you could.

Here are some ways to be a good citizen. One way is to send soldiers some drawings or games to the war. By doing that your making them happy. When i get older if i go to the war it would make me happy receiving things from kids. Not only kids but grownups can do it to. When i do this it makes me feel happy that I'm doing this for people who are helping this county but just not the county other things to. There are some ways to be a good citizen to.

What does it mean to be a good citizen, it means to work hard in school and helping people to get better at things. So when i grow up i can be smart and invent new things. When i work hard in school teachers wont have to worry about me. So when i get older there will be more things to do. There are some ways that you can be a good citizen.

How to be a good citizen: A couple ways to be a good citizen is to get involved with fun razors for schools or for sports. Also being a teacher for disability kids. All though your using time in your day its nice helping kids. And kids need help and when they don't get help then they will never learn. when you help kids they will all ways no your a good person. And those are some help full ways for being a good citizen.

If you want to be a good citizen you can do these things. You can participate in fun razors. Also try to help fun razors by buying cookies or what ever there sailing. Here are more things you can do. Like send pictures or other things to the war. And you can get a good education so your successful in life. When you smart you can invent things like to care cancer. When you care cancer you are helping a lot of people. And there are some ways that u could be a good citizen.

Narcisse

Have you ever wondered what it means to be a good citizen? As a sixth grader, here are some of my opinions on what makes up a good citizen. Some traits or qualities a good citizen should have are respecting people and their property. Being educated is another good trait, as is helping people less fortunate than you.

Good citizens should be kind to others by helping out when they can and respecting people's privacy and property; also by being kind and generous. A good citizen should be willing to help out. You could volunteer at an animal shelter or nursing home. Baby sitting kids or even animals is a great way to help out your neighbors or relatives. You could help out your school by tutoring, or do extra little jobs around your house to help out your mom or dad. There are tons of ways to help people out and these are just a few things you could do.

Good citizens need to be educated about things going on in the world. Illnesses and diseases are good things to know about, for they affect many people in the world. It's also good to be aware of weather and areas where hurricanes, tornadoes, and many other natural disasters affecting people around the globe; you could find out how you can donate money or help them out. Cultures and religions are great things to know about, because not a lot of people take the time to learn about cultures and religions different than their own. From India to Saudi Arabia to America there are so many different cultures and religions. Pollution and wars are good things to know about because they are things that affect the world and people every day. History and people who changed this county such as Albert Einstein, Martin Luther King Jr., and Benjamin Franklin have helped this world out so much. African Americans wouldn't be treated equally as white people without Martin Luther King Jr. We wouldn't have electricity without Benjamin Franklin, and Albert Einstein was smart and came up with the theory of relativity. These people were the building blocks of America as it is today, so they are very important to know. Finally the world and the people who inhabit it are very important issues to know about.

A good citizen should donate to needy people, also or people in disaster areas. You can help by having a garage sale or a bake sale to raise money. Fundraisers are great way to raise money. You could also get friends or other schools get involved. Maybe have a talent show or a play to raise money. Lemonade stands are great ways to raise money, especially on a hot day. Donating clothes and items are good ways to help. There are many ways to help out people and these are just a few ideas it is great to help people less fortunate than yourself so get INVOLVED! Well I hope some of my ideas as a 10th. grader told you some traits or qualities a good citizen should have, like being educated about the world, donating to be less fortunate than you. And by being kind and generous to anyone you meet.

Jose

I often wonder why people disrespect other people. Here are some good things that you and I could do to be a better citizen. For an example, we all should be respectful and helpful to older people. The men and women who fight for our country are the most honorable citizens. We should always show these men and women the highest respect. I believe that if all of us cared about each other and showed respect we wouldn't have as much hate and crime in the world.

I think that the men and women who fight in the war should get the highest respect. I think that honorable citizens should be respected. The honorable citizens that fight for our country should be treated with high respect. The men and women who serve for our country are honorable citizens. The people that fly the flag for America are good citizens. Showing honor and respect and giving equal treatment to all Americans and other people is being a good citizen.

A good citizen is showing respect, honor and giving equal treatment to everyone. Helping the elderly and young children are important in being a good citizen. I believe that if all of us loved each other and didn't fight we wouldn't have so much crime. Following the law and all rules and just helping someone else makes a difference. Being on a team and playing by the rules and just having fun. Win or lose, I try to enjoy each game I play I try to show good sportsmanship and try to set good examples. Listening and learning is important for our future so we can know how to help other generations.

Following the law and not fighting is being a good citizen. Being nice to different people than you is being a good citizen. Being happy and laughing and smiling when you show acts of kindness to everyone pass to other people and helps them to continue an act of kindness. Not getting mad and not arguing with people is being a good citizen. The things that you do should be done with common sense and honorable things so it will be not hurting someone else. What ever you choose to do, it should be something you are proud of, never ashamed of!

Being a good citizen is showing honor, leadership, respect and love. The world is full of people serving our country and these people die to defend our country. It's important for all of us to live each day with honor and respect and to treat everyone that we meet with kindness. Someone that doesn't treat people with respect is a bully. It's important to try everyday to treat people equally and you will be a good citizen.

Frank

Good citizens should help. No, have to help with things in this country or our land of the free is going to turn into the land of the bad. If we don't help, then there won't be anything we can do, but be sitting ducks for another country to take over. There are a lot of things that we can do but these are only some that we the people can do.

Good citizens get involved. Get into support groups to help those with loved ones in the war. Help groups for citizens that have loved ones that have died in the war. Participate in parades to honor those who have served and maybe died serving are country and saving other peoples life. Be in fundraisers to earn money for the soldiers to pay for necessary items like toilet paper, blankets, and food for them. Citizens join information groups to find things out before others, and to get the whole truth and nothing but the truth. If Saddam Hussein is captured then you want to know right? If there's an attack then you want to know right? If there's a victory you want to know right? Here are some other things you can do.

A good citizen donates to the Armed Forces. They need money for helmets. They need money for flack jackets so the soldiers don't get that hurt from shrapnel. They need money to pay people to make the bullets. They need money to pay people to make the guns. They need money to pay people to shoot the guns and make peace in the war. To make this money you as a citizen needs to help make the money they need to fight the war and win. They need donations to pay for it all. Now these are the last things that you can get ideas to help with the war.

Good citizens should help injured soldiers. Donate blood to injured soldiers. Maybe donate a useless organ to a soldier that really needs it. They need medical help so you should help. Some soldiers can't afford medical help. Some don't have enough time for medical help. Some don't know that they need medical help. So donate your time to becoming a doctor to help the soldiers that are hurt from fighting.

Good citizens get involved with the war. They also donate to the Armed Forces and try to help.

They help with medical things and also get educated. And that my friend is what a good citizen should do!

Pierre

If I want to be a good citizen I must be a part of my community. I could participate in local fund raisers and other charities. I would also need to learn about our government. Another way I could be a good citizen is by participating in patriotic events. All of these things make me a good citizen.

If I want to be a good citizen it would be good to get active in my community. I could participate in local fund raisers. I have been in the Relay for Life fund raiser for 2 years. I could also participate in can food drives. I have participated in my school's fund raiser can food drive every year so far. I could donate blood once I am 18. My Mom and Dad have both donated blood. I do all these things to get active in my community.

Another way I could be a good citizen is by getting involved. One way I get involved is to learn about democracy. Learning about democracy will help me vote when I get older. I could also get involved by learning about the war. I need to know about wars so that I can vote yes or no so that I know what to vote for. I can also contribute to the troops so the people defending others rights can get letters and items. Many people like getting letters from their home country. This is another way I can be a good citizen.

It is also good if I participate in patriotic events. I could participate in saying the Pledge of Allegiance. I say the pledge almost every day. I could volunteer to sing our national anthem at school assemblies. This would be one of the best ways to get active in my community. Its a good thing to celebrate the 4th of July which is the national U.S. birthday. These are all ways I could participate in patriotic events. There are many more ways to participate so I just listed a few.

I am a good citizen because I have done most of those things. I donated items and my time. I also study our government. I have also participated in many other activities including patriotic events. I like to be a good citizen and it opens a lot of opportunities for me.

Velasquez

As a 6th grader today, you can be a great citizen. Do you know how? Well I am going to tell you. One way you can be a good citizen is by supporting the troops. Another way is by knowing what's going on in the world. Third, you could help others who are in need. One way in which you can support the troops is sending letters, and letting them know how much you appreciate them. Something you might mention in your letter is how grateful you are, that because of them, our country is still free. Even though war is sad, there are times it is necessary to keep our homeland safe. Sending packages to the troops helps too. It is always nice to have things when you are away from home. You might ask them how they came to be in the military. What gives them the courage to fight for what they feel is right and true. I hope you learned a little more about being a good citizen by following the suggestions that I have mentioned.

Another way to be a good citizen is being interested in other people and the way they feel about things. Like their religion. How their beliefs differ from yours. Being sure you show them respect, even if you don't believe the same things. Another way you can find out about the world is from the newspaper. Reading about the things that are going on around you, and helping out when the need is there. Finding out what is happening right under your nose, perhaps in your own neighborhood. The last example is watching the news. You can learn a lot from the news and what's happening around you. These are simple ways in which you can be a great example and great citizen.

Finally, have you ever seen someone begging on the street corner? On the news there have been many natural disasters happening around the world. Do you know what you might do to help these people out? Well I am going to tell you. One way is to give them money. If you don't have an income, perhaps selling lemonade, or having a garage sale, would be a good way to earn money. Another way to help others in need would be to have a food drive, getting others involved in a good cause. Finally you could send letters of support and understanding to those who have lost so much. I hope you have learned how to be a good citizen in these 3 easy steps. Supporting our troops, trying to understanding the world in which we live, and helping people in need are all excellent ways of being a great citizen. Any or all of these things can be done, even if only 11 years old. I hope this may be of help to becoming a great citizen.

NANCY

Have you ever wondered what it means to be a good citizen? Do you feel like you won't be able to be a good citizen until you are older? Well, that's not true. People of all ages can be good citizens. Kids my age can volunteer in their community by picking up litter. They can be good citizens and support the troops by sending them letters, supplies, or food. When we get older and turn 18, we can vote. Voting is an important way to show that we are good citizens. It gives us the opportunity to choose the people and ideas that we think will be best for ourselves and our community.

Volunteering in the community is a good way for people of all ages to be good citizens. Picking up litter makes a community looks better, and it can bring money into the community. When picking up litter, we can collect bottles and cans and take them to a recycling center for money. The money can be donated to the city to help build something or do something to make the town a better place to live. Another good thing people can do is to go to a church in their town and volunteer to work in a soup kitchen and help cook and deliver warm meals to the needy. Volunteering to be a crossing guard is another good thing. By being a crossing guard, you can help children get to school safely each day. These are just some of the ways you can volunteer in your town or community.

Next I'm going to tell how to support our Troops. One way to support them is to buy a magnet for your car that says "Support Our Troops" on it. Another way to support the Troops would be to have a fundraiser. You can use the money collected to buy supplies and make care packages. Writing a letter to the Troops is another way to show support. We can write about how thankful we are for them, and how grateful we are that they are risking their lives to make things better. If you know someone who is fighting, you can send them pictures of you. These are good ways to support our Troops.

The last thing I'm going to talk about is voting. Voting is a way to choose what's right for a community. If a school needs to be fixed up or needs to be bigger, voting in an election is how we choose whether or not that is a good idea. Voting allows you to decide which people you want to be the leaders of your town or city. Voting allows people to choose whether or not they want to raise taxes or make better roads. If there is no place in your town for kids to play, bringing a group of people together and voting to build a park is another way. They can vote to decide if they should have a fundraiser, or go door to door to collect donations to build the park. These are good ways to vote.

There are many ways to be a good citizen. Listing them all would take forever. One of the things I talked about was to volunteer in your community. You could volunteer at a soup kitchen to help feed the needy. Another way was to support our Troops by sending letters or money for care packages. The last thing was voting in elections or as part of a group. If there is no park for your kids to play at you can start a fundraiser to build a park. These are all ways to be a good citizen.

Johnson

Do you know what it means to be a good citizen? It doesn't mean boring work. Here's some ways we can make it fun and entertaining. I know sometimes if I make a game out of doing something like picking up trash it makes it fun in the end.

Anybody can be a good citizen in my opinion. Older people, kids, and adults, we can all be good citizens. We don't all have to do the same things, different people can do different things. Kids like me could pick up trash. Older people could arrange things like community meetings. Adults could do the rest, like paint around the community, fix things that need to be repaired, weed gardens and mow lawns. If everybody worked together like that things would be great for the community. The town would look great, and people would be happy living there.

It doesn't have to be hard. It can be as simple as when your walking down the street and you pick up some trash. That's being a good citizen. Anybody old enough could do a paper route, or you could volunteer around the neighborhood. Things like painting birdhouses, gardening or raking leaves for the community, just however you can get involved. Maybe you or your friends could find something fun to do to help, or make it serious. It's your choice.

Even if you're new to the community, you can still get involved. All you have to is a few small things to make a big difference. Maybe you could create some way to make money for your community. Then you could use the money for things the community needs to buy. Even you can make a difference. It doesn't even have to be a big one. A small thing can be the start of a huge thing. For example, if you just pay for one pot of flowers, then somebody else buys a pot, and then somebody else and so on, then your community will have a huge garden filled with flowers because you made one small effort.

Now do you think you know what it means to be a good citizen? I think so. I've talked about how to make it fun to help out your community from the view of a sixth grader. I know there are ways to make it fun to be a good citizen.

Blair

It's important to be a good citizen. You can be kind to others, get involved in things, and do well in school.

One way to be a good person is to be nice to other people. Don't ever be mean to someone in front of or behind their back. Be kind and help people out. Always add encouragement. You can also be considerate to others. Pick up after yourself at home, and don't be lazy. Do your best to get along with siblings, and people you don't like.

Another way to be a good citizen is to get involved in things. Good sportsmanship is like good citizenship. So participate in clubs and sports. They're a good way to meet new people. You could also do jobs like babysitting, lawn mowing, dog walking, car washing, or other things to get money. Do odd jobs, or chores, around the house. Also get an allowance. Getting involved in whatever you can is a fun way of being a good citizen.

Getting a good education is another important way of becoming a good citizen. If you do well in school, then you have more opportunities for the future. It's important to try your hardest to get good grades. Always turn your work in on time, so you're on top of things. Then, it becomes easier to keep track of what you're doing. Also never give your teachers a hard time. Do what they tell you to do. If you try your hardest, then you can succeed.

Good citizens make the world a better place. You can be kind to others, get involved in things, and get a good education. But there are many other ways to be a good citizen.

Nay

You as a sixth grader can be a great citizen. Some ways you can be a good citizen are, be loyal to your country. Be good to your environment and finally get involved with the world.

One way you can be loyal to your country is to pledge to the flag with pride, knowing that we are free. Also you can prepare to grow-up to be in the Army, to keep our country even more free. You could plan to run for government too! You may also send fun letters, little things and food to troops that are away from there family serving for are freedom. Last you can help families with people serving for our freedom.

To help with the environment you could pick up litter. Make sure that you never litter. You can be good at recycling, like newspaper, plastic, metal etc. Instead of riding in a car, you could take your bike when possible. For every tree that you cut down, plant a new one. Don't destroy the forest by being careless with fire. Make sure you obey all the laws of the land.

People should be involved with their community and the world. You should watch the news. The news gives you details on the world's events. The newspaper is filled with even more details, and covers lots of different topics. There are many things in which you can get involved in just by reading the paper and being informed about the world around you.

These or all great things you can do to be a good citizen around your neighborhood, your community or even at home. I hope you enjoyed reading this paper on being a good citizen.

Fray

What is an awesome citizen you ask? In these three paragraphs you will read some really good ideas. To help out you can send packages to the soldiers in the war. You can also volunteer in your community. Also you can give money to the poor. In the following paragraphs I'll tell you even more ideas. What are you waiting for read these paragraphs!

If you don't think we need to send packages, then you're wrong. Here are some reasons why we need to. One reason is in the war the soldiers don't have everything we have in our life. They would probably like it if you sent them something. In the package you could put a picture of their family. I bet they could use soap too. You can do your part if you sent them something. I hope you now know why they need something. If you don't have anything to send, write them a letter.

Another idea is to volunteer in your community. I'm going to give you some ideas. First, you could help clean your neighborhood park if you have one. You could raise money to help send the soldiers in the war gifts. You could read to younger kids who don't know how to read yet. There are a whole bunch of other things you could do too. I hope you want to go out and help out in your community.

If you still don't want to use any of those ideas I just gave you, here's another idea. You can give money to the poor. Here are some reasons why. The poor don't have stuff like you and me. Sometimes when you see them they look very cold. They can be really hungry too. Some of them even live on the streets.

Now I hope you know what a good citizen is. Just to make sure, I'll summarize what I just said. I just told you to send packages to the soldiers fighting in the war. I also suggested that you could volunteer in your community. Last but not least you can give money to the poor. Now that you know how to be a good citizen, go and help out right now (unless you're in school)!

Beal

How would you like to learn to be the best citizen ever? Well first you could start a fundraiser. Second, you could start a family support group. Finally, you could help people in your class to make sure they get a good education. Now here's more detail about these topics.

To help with the war effort you can raise money like a fundraiser. One type of fundraiser you could do is having a lemonade stand. Another fundraiser would be to ask a company for a donation for the war effort. Once you've done a fundraiser you can send it to the government and make sure to tell them it's for the war effort so they don't think somebody sent their taxes. I would do this if I was you, and it would so much if you participated. The war needs as much help as they can get. My goal is get $200 dollars to give to the war. Millions of other people are helping why can't you.

Another way of being a good citizen is you can make or join a family support group. A family support group helps families who are depressed or are really mad. Once you've joined or started a family support group you can ease people who are very mad and try and make it so they don't take it out on other people. For people who are depressed try and make them look at the brighter part things, happy things instead of sad things. If you have them look at the brighter part of things they won't be so depressed all the time.

The final way of becoming a good citizen is by helping any and everyone to make sure they get a good education. To help make sure the get a good education is by helping them with their homework so they get a good grade on it. If they struggle with a question don't ell them the answer or they won't learn anything, so help them with the question but remember don't tell them. Another way is by becoming a tutor to help more than one or two kids who struggle, you can help many. If they need to study give them this tip, make study cards to help them remember what the answers are. If you have an older sibling ask them for help and if you don't ask your parents to help you. I'd try and help people who want help. I strongly advise that you do this.

These three ways are the best in the world try them you'll see. You'll see that our ideas are #1 instead of #2. These are world-class hints to becoming rich and kind. It's all-free. I would defiantly take this opportunity if I were you.

JONAS

Have you ever wondered what it means to be a good citizen? Well if you haven't I am going to tell you right now. It means to help people across streets. It also means to get involved with the people around you. Then finally it means to help clean up your community. Now if your keep reading you will understand.

You can help out with community service. You can help clean up cans and cigarette butts and also just garbage off the side of the road. You can help clean up parks in your neighbor hood. You can also help clean up the beaches around your house. You can also just try cleaning up you school and not disrespecting school property. You can help out at a soup kitchen. You can also help out people who are mentally challenged.

In order to be a good citizen you need to get involved with the people around you and in your neighbor hoods. You can help out in your community library. You could babysit kids on short notice. You could help out people with groceries. You could start neighbor hood meetings. You could start a club that would help support our troops. You could also help donate things to human and animal shelters.

Also in order to be a good citizen you could help people cross streets. You could help little kids across streets on your way to school. You could also help people with groceries if they need it. You could help people if they drop things. Then you could help with fundraisers.

So did you wonder what being a good citizen meant? Well if you did I Hope you know now. I told you that you have to help people cross streets. You have to get involved with the people around you. So get off your butt and start doing some good for your community.

BLAISE

As a sixth grade being a good citizen is an important part of my life. Sure you are probably thinking, why is it important to you? Well being a good citizen isn't just about keeping your community clean. For example helping others makes you a good citizen. Also learning about diseases.

Last but not least supporting the troops. There are many more but I am not going to list them. I t would take up to much space.

Who is a good citizen? A good citizen is someone who helps others. I mean if some guy is sitting on the street asking for money you don't half to tell him he can live with you. I f you can give him a few bucks. That is one way you can be a good citizen. A good citizen is someone who picks up after themselves and others. I f you are in the park eating lunch throw your trash away. Also if some other person was eating there lunch and they didn't throw there garbage away throw it away. That is another way to be a good citizen. A good citizen is someone who respects their elders and is kind. If you are taking a jog and you run I into someone say sorry or excuse me. Also if you are talking to your parents and they tell you to do something. Do it, don't make them half to tell you again. That is how you can be a good citizen.

Another way to be a good citizen is to learn about diseases. Well until just recently I didn't know anything about diseases. Then I wanted to know. So I learned. I learned about what they did to you. How you get them. What you can do to prevent them. I learned lots of things. So if you want know these things than learn. Be a good citizen.

Last but not least you can support the troops. The troops are out half way across the world away from their families. So when you see them on TV doesn't just say that they are trying to be heroes. They are heroes. So when they come home appreciate them be proud of them. In a way they are protecting you so support them and you can be a good citizen.

I have just told you ways you can be a good citizen. So use them.

SCHNEIDER

Here are some good ways for me to be a good citizen. The first way for me to be a good citizen is to support the troops. The next way for me to be a good citizen is to follow the law or rules. The last way for me to be a good citizen is to donate to the poor. And that is what I'm going to be telling you in this essay.

A way I could be a good citizen is, I should follow the law or rules. The first way I could follow the rules is, I can do my chores so it will make my mom happy. The next way I could follow the rules is to do my homework. The last way for me to follow the rules is to not get in trouble at school. The first way to follow the law is to not do drugs. The last way for me to follow the law is to not drink. And those are some ways for me to follow the rules or law.

A way for me to be a good citizen is to support the troops. The first way for me to support the troops is to send them stuff like letters, chocolates, and cards. The next way I could support the troops is I could buy stuff to show that I support them like magnets wristbands, bracelets, and other stuff. The last way I could support the troops is, I could keep up with the war by reading newspapers and watching the news. And those are ways I could support the troops and be a good citizen.

The last way for me to be a good citizen is I could donate to the poor. The first thing I could donate to the poor is food, for example, canned foods. The next thing I could donate to the poor is water, juice, or any other type of drinkable products. The last thing I could donate to the poor is clothes like shirts, pants, shoes, or socks. The way this makes me a good citizen is I'm donating to people less fortunate than me. And those are some ways to donate to the poor and be a good citizen.

These are a couple of ways for me to be a good citizen. The first way is I could support the troops. The next way I could be a good citizen is I could follow the law or rules. The last way for me to be a good citizen is to donate to the poor. And that is my essay on how to be a good citizen.

What Does it Mean to Be a Good Citizen?

Anita

Do you know what it takes to be a good citizen? Even if you think being a good citizen is hard to be, it really isn't. All you have to do is make good choices and help in the community. You can learn, care about, and know what it feels like to be a true citizen. Have fun learning.

Many people know what some things are and what things aren't, but it never hurts to know more than what you know already! Kids can learn what war things are by learning. Learn where different wars take place. They can also learn about diseases that can harm you. There are many different diseases that people know of that can harm you. One last thing that you or someone else can learn is, who people are and what they can do to you. There are many other ways to help.

Children can help the war by being a good citizen. Kids can run fundraisers and donations for things needed for the war. There are ways to collect money too! They can send the men and women, which fight for our country, food, drinks, candy, coffee, letters or thank you notes. Everyone can help! Kids can also help by reading the newspaper and listening to the radio or television. When reading the newspaper, you can read what's going on in the world and war. You can also make good choices about how your life should go. There are also other ways to be a good citizen other than making good choices.

Kids can become educated about the war going on. They can learn about the war itself. Many may learn about the war and might join it. Kids can learn how the war was wedged into our lives. They can learn how our government works. You can have someone teach yourself to learn about what is going on. Kids can be a someone today, and a hero tomorrow!

Hopefully you learned a few things about being a good citizen. You have learned that learning can help you consider yourself as a good citizen. Maybe you have also learned that being in the action by helping out can be very caring, on my standards at least. Another thing you could have read was, that being yourself can also help in various ways. Although you have heard of other ways to help, you can still learn more ways to be a good citizen.

When I think of a good citizen, I think of a person who dose great things For their community. Someone who tryst to make his or her comity a wonderful place for them and the people of their comity A person who can take lead and finish what has to be done and brings the community together to do things that will improve the community.

A good citizen is a person who takes his or her time to help others . Such as Fire Fighters, Police Officers and army men and women Also a good citizen will strive to do good for their community . Good Citizens help those in need. They help the poor, angered and sake.

Many great people become very respected citizens of their community. As respected citizens they should sit an example for their community. A citizen should be involved whit their community. Such as starting groups for kid, funds and can drives. Also a good citizen should be ready to those in need. Citizens should do as much good as needed or possible. They can organize a plan to clean a river, pike up trash from a park.

Other things a citizen can do is give eve very student a good education, also they can help care for the sick. If you need examples of a good citizen hear are some .You have your local Fire Fighters who great citizens because they work very hard at saving lives and keeping fires from spreading. Also another good citizen is your local army men and women are great citizens because they risk their lives for there community and their country. Even your teachers, P.T.A, jointers, prince able and other citizens who take there own time to help others. So now you know that it doesn't matter who the person is but yet they are a great citizen.

So now you know whom I think a good citizen is to bewitch is a person who takes care of their community .Now that I have told you everything I think a good citizen is you should of what a good citizen is.

JUST FOR THE RECORD I WANTED TO PRINT THE STUDENTS WORKS AS THEY WERE. PLEASE FORGIVE SOME ERRORS, HOWEVER THEY DID A GREAT JOB.

1. Here are a few qualities that a good citizen possesses:
2. Respect and demand respect from a fellow citizen
3. Will not destroy public and or private properties
4. Will not abandon their countries
5. Will not betray their countries
6. Love and respect their countries and the laws

Abide by all the laws and governments as long as they are fair and just.

First part of reeducation is dismantling the school system for a year. For that year every citizen is required to attend civic schools which will be held by the Education facilitator in conjunction with the Army and the Police. At the end of that every citizen young and old will be granted a *certificate* with a number and without that number you will not be admitted to any schools, get a visa, get married, get a job and even get credit.

Certification refers to the confirmation of certain characteristics of an object, person, or organization. This confirmation is often, but not always, provided by some form of external review, education, or assessment.

One of the most common types of certification in modern society is professional certification, where a person is certified as being able to competently complete a job or task, usually by the passing of an examination.

There are two general types of professional certification: some are valid for lifetime, once the exam is passed. Others have to be recertified again after a certain period of time. Also, certifications can differ within a profession by the level or specific area of expertise they refer to. For example, in IT Industry there are different certifications available for Software Tester, Project Manager, and Developer. Similarly, the Joint Commission on Allied Health Personnel in Ophthalmology offers three certifications in the same profession, but with increasing complexity.

Certification does not refer to the state of legally being able to practice or work in a profession. That is *licensure*. Usually, licensure is administered by a governmental entity for public protection purposes and certification by a professional association. However, they are similar in that they both require the demonstration of a certain level of knowledge or ability.

The other most common certification refers to the confirmation of certain characteristics of an object, person, or organization. This confirmation is often, but not always, provided by some form of external review, education, or assessment.

One of the most common types of certification in modern society is professional certification, where a person is certified as being able to competently complete a job or task, usually by the passing of an examination.

There are two general types of professional certification: some are valid for lifetime, once the exam is passed. Others have to be recertified again after a certain period of time. Also, certifications can differ within a profession by the level or specific area of expertise they refer to. For example, in IT Industry there are different certifications available for Software Tester, Project Manager, and Developer. Similarly, the Joint Commission on Allied Health Personnel in

Ophthalmology offers three certifications in the same profession, but with increasing complexity.

Certification does not refer to the state of legally being able to practice or work in a profession. That is licensure. Usually, licensure is administered by a governmental entity for public protection purposes and certification by a professional association. However, they are similar in that they both require the demonstration of a certain level of knowledge or ability.

The other most common type of certification in modern society is product certification. This refers to processes intended to determine if a product meets minimum standards, similar to quality assurance.

Organizational certification, such as the Earthcheck environmental and sustainability certification, is usually referred to as accreditation. The differentiation in terms is especially relevant with regards to the National Commission for Certifying Agencies (NCCA), which is a body that accredits certifying organizations.

Earthcheck benchmarking and certification complies with the Intergovernmental Panel for Climate Change (IPCC) Guidelines for National Greenhouse Gas Inventories, the World Business Council for Sustainable Development (WBCSD) Greenhouse Gas Protocol, and the International Organization for Standardization (ISO) 14064 range of standards for greenhouse gas accounting.

This refers to processes intended to determine if a product meets minimum standards, similar to quality assurance.

Organizational certification, such as the Earthcheck environmental and sustainability certification, is usually referred to as accreditation. The differentiation in terms is especially relevant with regards to the National Commission for Certifying Agencies (NCCA), which is a body that accredits certifying organizations.

Earthcheck benchmarking and certification complies with the Intergovernmental Panel for Climate Change (IPCC) Guidelines for National Greenhouse Gas Inventories, the World Business Council for Sustainable Development (WBCSD) Greenhouse Gas Protocol, and the International Organization for Standardization (ISO) 14064 range of standards for greenhouse gas accounting.

For every twenty miles there should be hospital, a school, a police precinct, a fire department, a library and a park. All of them should be working together because all of them have a responsibility in shaping kids who are the future and who are expected to be of great moral and morale.

A major problem with morality is that if no one claims responsibility for deciding and acting out the ethical principles of right and wrong, morality becomes a word without meaning. Morality is a system of principles or rules of conduct to which humans conform. Presently our "wider culture" exemplifies the debasement of rules of conduct with little common agreement as to what rules or principles we should be following. Is this perhaps because religion in general no longer can be considered the one true source of morality? The continuing revelations of sexual abuse within some religious institutions are of course part of the sad state of affairs. A well-known, but little understood story in the first chapters of the Bible regarding the Garden of Eden and two special trees in that garden sheds light on our current moral crisis. Unfortunately, this is unlikely to prove an effective answer. Until we are prepared to acknowledge a common source of morality that lies outside of human reason, there will be no improvement in the moral crisis that envelopes our cultures. They are expected to put country first. Country comes before personal gain.

The country should be divided into states or communes with its own sub-flag with the country main flag on top. That would promote competition against communes, which would benefit the whole country. Economic competition takes place in markets—meeting grounds of intending suppliers and buyers.1 Typically, a few sellers compete to attract favorable offers from prospective buyers. Similarly, intending buyers compete to obtain good offers from suppliers. When a contract is concluded, the buyer and seller exchange PROPERTY RIGHTS in a good, service, or asset. Everyone interacts voluntarily, motivated by self-interest.

In the process of such interactions, much information is signaled through prices. Keen sellers cut prices to attract buyers, and buyers reveal their preferences by raising their offers to out-compete other buyers. When a deal is done, no one may be entirely happy with the agreed price, but both contract partners feel better off. If prices exceed costs, sellers make a profit, an inducement to SUPPLY more. When other competitors learn what actions lead to PROFITS, they may emulate the original supplier. Conversely, losses tell suppliers what to abandon or modify.

Suppliers also engage in non-price competition. They try to improve their products to gain a competitive advantage over their rivals. To this end, they incur the costs and risks of product INNOVATION. This type of competition has inspired innumerable evolutionary steps—between the Wright brothers' first fence hopper and the latest Boeing 747, for example. Such competition has driven unprecedented material progress since the INDUSTRIAL REVOLUTION.

Differentiated products may give pioneering suppliers a "market niche." Such a niche is never entirely secure, however, since other competitors will strive to improve their own products, keeping all suppliers in a state of "creative unease."

Another tool of competition is process innovation to lower costs, which allows producers to undercut competitors on price. This kind of competitive action has given us ubiquitous two-dollar pocket calculators only a generation after the first calculators sold for three hundred times that price!

A third instrument to out-compete one's rivals is ADVERTISING to bring one's wares to buyers' attention. Suppliers also compete by offering warranties and after-sales services. This is common with complicated, durable products such as cars. It reduces the buyer's transaction costs and strengthens the supplier's competitive position.

Competition thus obliges people to remain alert and incur costs. Before one can compete effectively in a market, one needs the relevant knowledge. Buyers need to ask themselves what their requirements are, what products are available, what they can afford, and how various products compare, taking prices into account. This imposes search costs—think of the time and effort involved in buying a house, for example. Suppliers have to find out where there is, what technical attributes people want in their product, where to obtain the many inputs and components, how to train workers, how to distribute their wares, how to improve products and processes, how competitors will react, and much more. Such efforts—in research, development, and marketing—may be very costly and may still come to naught. For every market bonanza, there are many disappointments. And other costs arise as sellers and buyers negotiate contract details and monitor and enforce delivery.

In a dynamic, specialized economy, the costs of searching for knowledge and carrying out exchanges (called "transaction costs") tend to be high. Therefore, it is not surprising that market participants are keen to reduce transaction costs and associated risks. One method is to agree on set rules (called "institutions") that help them to economize on knowledge acquisition costs. Markets fulfill people's aspirations more effectively when there are enforced and expedient rules. Another transaction cost–saving device is to agree on open-ended, long-term relationships, such as employment contracts. Yet another is advertising, a means for sellers to inform buyers and save them some search costs. Deal making is also facilitated by intermediaries—market experts such as brokers, realtors and auctioneers.

Despite these methods of reducing transaction costs, competition is uncomfortable and costly to competitors. Some entrepreneurs enjoy the market rivalry per se. But most people are ambivalent about competition in a particular way; they would like to avoid competing on their own side of the market, but welcome competition among those they buy from or sell to. In a free society, people are, of course, entitled to rest on their laurels by not competing, but they will lose market share, and their assets will probably lose value. Moreover, each commune or state is in charge of its infrastructure, tax-collection, and its law under the guide of the supreme councils. Each facilitator meets twice a month with both the supreme council members and the populace in order to show in details the progress of their communes. If a facilitator is not showing immediate progress he or she will be removed as quickly as possible. Moreover, all facilitators in a commune and other communes should be working together for the better advancement of the country. They have to have good *communication* among themselves.

Good communication skills are skills that facilitate people to communicate effectively with one another. Effectual communication engages the choice of the best communications channel, the technical know-how to use the channel, the presentation of information to the target audience, and the skill to understand responses received from others. Self development, interpersonal skills, mutual understanding, mutual cooperation and trust is also important to set a complete channel of most effective and winning communication skills.

There are mainly three types of communication skills, expressive skills, listening skills and skills for managing the overall process of communication. The basic fundamental of all these types of communication is emotional skills.

Expressive skills are required to convey message to others through words, facial expressions and body language. Listening skills are skills that are used to obtain messages or information from others. These help to clearly understand what a person feels and thinks about you or understand the other person closely. Skills for managing the overall process of communication help to recognize the required information and develop a strong hold on the existing rules of communication and interaction.

Importance of communication skills can never be ignored or neglected. These skills are the key to executing good management skills. With good management skills, you can have a team of members who together create an ambience of open communication, concise messages, probe for clarifications, recognize nonverbal signals, and mutual understanding. Good communication involves a set of complex skills.

The modern world today, calls for high scale effective communication skills in order to win the heavy competition in all spheres of life. For effective communication, a sender transmits his or her message in a clear and organized form to maintain and promote the need and interest of the receivers. Receivers or listeners show interest only if the person communicating is loaded with confidence, gestures and softness. Apart from management professionals, good communication skills are also required at all stages of life.

A good government should be promoting interracial marriages and inter-economic or inter-class marriages. A good way to promote these marriages is by giving them tax-break. A tax break is a tax saving. This includes: * Tax exemption, an exemption from all or certain taxes of a state or nation in which part of the taxes that would normally be collected from an individual or an organization are instead foregone In one word, an awesome government or a country that needs to prosper should be fighting for race and economic equalities.

> It is hard to overstate the consequences of choosing more of the same -- the very policies that have sundered our social contract. But hear the judgment of Nobel laureate Kenneth Arrow, echoing Martin Luther King Jr.'s life and martyrdom. "The vast inequalities of income weaken a society's sense of mutual concern," Arrow said. "... The sense that we are all members of the social order is vital to the meaning of civilization Remember that Martin Luther King had a dream and that dream is that one day "all races can live together in harmony. Every married couple should be urged to attend a seminar every three years. The same way lawyers, doctors, teachers refresh their skills by attending workshops every married couple needs to refresh their love in order to avoid divorce and chaos. The government should give each couple who attends these seminars a special stipend in the form of food stamps or monetary values.

Anthropologists have proposed several competing definitions of marriage so as to encompass the wide variety of marital practices observed across cultures. In his book *The History of Human Marriage* (1921), Edvard Westermarck defined marriage as "a more or less durable connection between male and female lasting beyond the mere act of propagation till after the birth of the offspring." In *The Future of Marriage in Western Civilization* (1936), he rejected his earlier definition, instead provisionally defining marriage as "a relation of one or more men to one or more women that is recognised by custom or law".

The anthropological handbook *Notes and Queries* (1951) defined marriage as "a union between a man and a woman such that children born to the woman are the recognized legitimate offspring of both partners." In recognition of a practice by the Nuer of Sudan allowing women to act as a husband in certain circumstances, Kathleen Gough suggested modifying this to "a woman and one or more other persons."

Edmund Leach criticized Gough's definition for being too restrictive in terms of recognized legitimate offspring and suggested that marriage be viewed in terms of the different types of rights it serves to establish. Leach expanded the definition and proposed that "Marriage is a relationship established between a woman and one or more other persons, which provides that a child born to the woman under circumstances not prohibited by the rules of the relationship, is accorded full birth-status rights common to normal members of his society or social stratum. Leach argued that no one definition of marriage applied to all cultures. He offered a list of ten rights associated with marriage, including sexual monopoly and rights with respect to children, with specific rights differing across cultures.

Duran Bell also criticized the legitimacy-based definition on the basis that some societies do not require marriage for legitimacy, arguing that in societies where illegitimacy means only that the mother is unmarried and has no other legal implications, a legitimacy-based definition of marriage is circular. He proposed defining marriage in terms of sexual access rights. The modern English word "marriage" derives from Middle English *mariage*, which first appears in 1250–1300 C.E. This in turn is derived from Old French *marier* (to marry) and ultimately Latin *marītāre* (to marry) and *marītus* (of marriage).

Every religion has to be respected. Everyone is free to practice every religion that they so desire. *King wrote this paper for Davis's Philosophy of Religion course. In the essay, which is largely drawn from D. Miall Edwards's The Philosophy of Religion, King examines various philosophical and anthropological arguments for the origin of religion. The word "race" in the title refers to the human race, not a particular group. Davis gave King an A and praised his "thoughtful, critical analysis.*

The question of the origin of religion in the human race still remains one of the insoluble mysteries confronting the mind of man. Men have attempted to solve this problem through scientific research, only to find that the results lead to inevitable antinomies. Like all other questions of "origins," the origin of religion is more a matter of speculation than of investigation; or to make it less extreme, it will at all events be admitted that speculation is involved in a problem for which an entirely satisfactory solution cannot be found through historical investigation alone. We may trace a particular religion to its faint beginnings, we may even be able to determine the features which the most primitive form of religion presents, but we shall still be far from furnishing an answer to the question--How did religion arise? What is its source?

It is significant that the question of the origin of religion was not scientifically studied until modern times. Before we come to consider some modern theories it may be well to refer briefly to two views which were once widely prevalent, but which are now obsolete or at least absolescent.1

Jewish, Christian, and Mohammedan theologians, for a long time, assumed Divine Revelation as a necessary factor in the rise of religion, either in the form of a primitive Revelation vouchsafed to all mankind, or of a special Revelation to certain peoples singled out for the purpose. This view has usually taken the form of a belief in a primeval monotheism of divine origin, from which polytheism in its many forms is a later relapse. It is now usually held that the doctrine of revelation has explained the origin of religion in far too intellectual and mechanical a fashion, "as if religion began with the impartation to man of a set of ideas, ready-made and finished ideas poured into a mind conceived as a kind of empty vessel."\[Footnote:] D. Maill Edwards, The Philosophy of Religion. This is a crudely un psychological view.2 Moreover, the theory of evolution has led us to conceive of primitive man as utterly incapable of receiving and retaining the highly developed ideas which primitive revelation was supposed to communicate to him. Voodoo, witchcraft, sorcery or worshiping any idols or saints and every other kind of magic should be illegal because they do not help the growth of any society in any form or shape. If anyone is caught practicing any one of the above he or she will be prosecuted to the fullest extent of the law.

Every citizen upon completion of high school or has reached his eighteenth birthday should be enlisted in the country's armed forces for a minimum of two years with option to make it a career.

On the campaign trail Barack Obama acknowledged our dangerous shortfall in military recruiting but proposed no effective remedy; his program for national service - focused on environmentalism instead of the military - will do nothing to replenish our perilously over-stretched armed forces.

The United States needs a bigger army. If eternal vigilance is the price of liberty, it is a price that should be paid by all - and that requires national service. The draft is essential for achieving victory in the long war on Islamist fascism and assuring our capacity to meet the many other threats that are likely to emerge in this already dangerous twenty-first century.

A military draft is well within the American tradition, and the scars of the Vietnam-era draft should not keep us from doing what our national interest requires. During the Vietnam War the draft became not a symbol of unity but of division. The reason was simple: the draft became unpopular because the war became unpopular.

The draft should not be viewed as an instrument to force citizens to fight an unpopular war. As was the case during both world wars, the draft is effective at marshalling needed manpower to fight wars that society, by general consensus, deems just and necessary. It also helps to stimulate volunteers who might need that extra incentive to step up and answer the call to duty.

But the primary reason for reinstituting the draft is this: our military needs it. Between 1990 and 2000, the Army shrank by a quarter of a million troops. The Navy, the Air Force, and the Marine Corps had their manpower reduced by 36 percent, 34 percent, and 12 percent, respectively.

Despite all our technological advantages, troop strength matters. Even the addition of just 20,000 to 30,000 troops in Iraq during the "surge" completely changed the complexion of the conflict. In the second half of 2007, after the surge reached its full force, violence in Iraq declined by 60 percent, forcing even Democratic congressman Jack Murtha, a die-hard opponent of the Iraq War, to admit that the surge was working.

There's no substitute for boots on the ground. The lack of available ground troops has led some officials and analysts to conclude that if the United States found another unavoidable military conflict, we would have to rely on air power and even, if it was serious enough, nuclear weapons. We must face the reality that, given our current international commitments, and the likelihood that these commitments will grow, we will need a bigger army than our current all-volunteer force.

National service is a call to renew the self-sacrifice, patriotism, and stoicism that once animated our country, but that today seem too often shelved in favor of a self-centered veneration of personal happiness. Yes, national service would be a costly endeavor and would undoubtedly provoke libertarian outrage from a number of eighteen-year-olds who've become estranged from the very idea of a citizen's obligation to his country.

But the question is this: is enlarging America's military to defend our vital national interests and renew our sense of national unity worth the price of a national service program? The answer is undeniably yes. More than that, it's inevitable, if we are to survive and prosper as a free and independent nation.

The rights of animals should be respected and should be treated with dignity. So in the police force there should be officers whose sole job is to protect animals from being abused. When someone is caught mistreating animals, that person should be in the headlines to avoid others from abusing animals.

Using animals in research and to test the safety of products has been a topic of heated debate for decades. According to data collected by F. Barbara Orlans for her book, *In the Name of Science: Issues in Responsible Animal Experimentation,* sixty percent of all animals used in testing are used in biomedical research and product-safety testing (62). People have different feelings for animals; many look upon animals as companions while others view animals as a means for advancing medical techniques or furthering experimental research. However individuals perceive animals, the fact remains that animals are being exploited by research facilities and cosmetics companies all across the country and all around the world. Although humans often benefit from successful animal research, the pain, the suffering, and the deaths of animals are not worth the possible human benefits. Therefore, animals should not be used in research or to test the safety of products.

First, animals' rights are violated when they are used in research. Tom Regan, a philosophy professor at North Carolina State University, states: "Animals have a basic moral right to respectful treatment. . . .This inherent value is not respected when animals are reduced to being mere tools in a scientific experiment" (qtd. in Orlans 26). Animals and people are alike in many ways; they both feel, think, behave, and experience pain. Thus, animals should be treated with the same respect as humans. Yet animals' rights are violated when they are used in research because they are not given a choice. Animals are subjected to tests that are often painful or cause permanent damage or death, and they are never given the option of *not* participating in the experiment. Regan further says, for example, that "animal [experimentation] is morally wrong no matter how much humans may benefit because the animal's basic right has been infringed. Risks are not morally transferable to those who do not choose to take them" (qtd. in Orlans 26). Animals do not willingly sacrifice themselves for the advancement of human welfare and new technology. Their decisions are made for them because they cannot vocalize their own preferences and choices. When humans decide the fate of animals in research environments, the animals' rights are taken away without any thought of their well-being or the quality of their lives. Therefore, animal experimentation should be stopped because it violates the rights of animals.

Next, the pain and suffering that experimental animals are subject to is not worth any possible benefits to humans. "The American Veterinary Medial Association defines animal pain as an unpleasant sensory and emotional experience perceived as arising from a specific region of the body and associated with actual or potential tissue damage" (Orlans 129). Animals feel pain in many of the same ways that humans do; in fact, their reactions to pain are virtually identical (both humans and animals scream, for example). When animals are used for product toxicity testing or laboratory research, they are subjected to painful and frequently deadly experiments. Two of the most commonly used toxicity tests are the Draize test and the LD50 test, both of which are infamous for the intense pain and suffering they inflect upon experimental animals. In the Draize test the substance or product being tested is placed in the eyes of an animal (generally a rabbit is used for this test); then the animal is monitored for damage to the cornea and other tissues in and near the eye. This test is intensely painful for the animal, and blindness, scarring, and death are generally the end results. The Draize test has been criticized for being unreliable and a needless waste of animal life. The LD50 test is used to test the dosage of a substance that is necessary to cause death in fifty percent of the animal subjects within a certain amount of time. To perform this test, the researchers hook the animals up to tubes that pump huge amounts of the test product into their stomachs until they die. This test is extremely painful to the animals because death can take days or even weeks. According to Orlans, the animals suffer from "vomiting, diarrhea, paralysis, convulsion, and internal bleeding. Since death is the required endpoint, dying animals are not put out of their misery by euthanasia" (154). In his article entitled "Time to Reform Toxic Tests," Michael Balls, a professor of medial cell biology at the University of Nottingham and chairman of the trustees of FRAME (the Fund for the Replacement of Animals in Medical Experiments), states that the LD50 test is "scientifically unjustifiable. The precision it purports to provide is an illusion because of uncontrollable biological variables" (31). The use of the Draize test and the LD50 test to examine product toxicity has decreased over the past few years, but these tests have not been eliminated completely. Thus, because animals are subjected to agonizing pain, suffering and death when they are used in laboratory and cosmetics testing, animal research must be stopped to prevent more waste of animal life.

Finally, the testing of products on animals is completely unnecessary because viable alternatives are available. Many cosmetic companies, for example, have sought better ways to test their products without the use of animal subjects. In *Against Animal Testing*, a pamphlet published by The Body Shop, a well-known cosmetics and bath-product company based in London, the development of products that "use natural ingredients, like bananas and Basil nut oil, as well as others with a long history of safe human usage" is advocated instead of testing on animals (3). Furthermore, the Draize test has become practically obsolete because of the development of a synthetic cellular tissue that closely resembles human skin. Researchers can test the potential damage that a product can do to the skin by using this artificial "skin" instead of testing on animals. Another alternative to this test is a product called Eyetex. This synthetic material turns opaque when a product damages it, closely resembling the way that a real eye reacts to harmful substances. Computers have also been used to simulate and estimate the potential damage that a product or chemical can cause, and human tissues and cells have been used to examine the effects of harmful substances. In another method, *in vitro* testing, cellular tests are done inside a test tube. All of these tests have been proven to be useful and reliable alternatives to testing products on live animals. Therefore, because effective means of product toxicity testing are available without the use of live animal specimens, testing potentially deadly substances on animals is unnecessary.

However, many people believe that animal testing is justified because the animals are sacrificed to make products safer for human use and consumption. The problem with this reasoning is that the animals' safety, well-being, and quality of life is generally not a consideration. Experimental animals are virtually tortured to death, and all of these tests are done in the interest of human welfare, without any thought to how the animals are treated. Others respond that animals themselves benefit from animal research. Yet in an article entitled "Is Your Experiment Really Necessary?" Sheila Silcock, a research consultant for the RSPCA, states: "Animals may themselves be the beneficiaries of animal experiments. But the value we place on the quality of their lives is determined by their perceived value to humans" (34). Making human's lives better should not be justification for torturing and exploiting animals. The value that humans place on their own lives should be extended to the lives of animals as well.

Still other people think that animal testing is acceptable because animals are lower species than humans and therefore have no rights. These individuals feel that animals have no rights because they lack the capacity to understand or to knowingly exercise these rights. However, animal experimentation in medical research and cosmetics testing cannot be justified on the basis that animals are lower on the evolutionary chart than humans since animals resemble humans in so many ways. Many animals, especially the higher mammalian species, possess internal systems and organs that are identical to the structures and functions of human internal organs. Also, animals have feelings, thoughts, goals, needs, and desires that are similar to human functions and capacities, and these similarities should be respected, not exploited, because of the selfishness of humans. Tom Regan asserts that "animals are subjects of a life just as human beings are, and a subject of a life has inherent value. They are . .

. ends in themselves" (qtd. in Orlans 26). Therefore, animals' should be respected because they have an inherent right to be treated with dignity. The harm that is committed against animals should not be minimized because they are not considered to be "human."

In conclusion, animal testing should be eliminated because it violates animals' rights, it causes pain and suffering to the experimental animals, and other means of testing product toxicity are available. Humans cannot justify making life better for themselves by randomly torturing and executing thousands of animals per year to perform laboratory experiments or to test products. Animals should be treated with respect and dignity, and this right to decent treatment is not upheld when animals are exploited for selfish human gain. After all, humans are animals too.

Talk about parental responsibility. The California Senate just passed a bill that could send parents to jail for up to a year if their kids -- from kindergarten through eighth grade -- miss too much school.

Senate Bill 1317 is actually a public safety measure, according to State Sen. Mark Leno (D-San Francisco), because children who don't attend school regularly or drop out early are more likely to turn to crime. "Three-quarters of our state inmate population are high school dropouts," Leno was quoted as saying.

Parents whose kids miss too much school could be subject to up to a year in jail and a $2,000 fine, though judges could put the punishment on hold to give parents a chance to get their kids to class.

The Fresno Bee reported that the bill would apply to parents or guardians of children age 6 or older in kindergarten through eighth grade.

To find someone guilty under the bill, prosecutors would have to prove that the parents failed to reasonably supervise and encourage the student to attend school. How much school is too much school to miss?

Chronic truancy would be as missing 10 percent or more of the school year without a valid excuse. The bill is the brainchild of San Francisco District Attorney Kamala Harris, who is seeking the Democratic nomination for attorney general.

> Parents will be held accountable if their children do not attend school. So the Education facilitator's office should have its own Police force to ensure that every child is getting a free and fair education. Every child can learn and that should be any school's motto.

I believe that every child can learn and has the right to a solid education. I believe students learn best when they are a part of the educational process and feel safe while learning. They should have enjoyment and power, to some extent, in their educational experience. Giving children some control of their learning makes the process more personable and meaningful. Children should be encouraged to voice their opinions in a democratic and respectful manner. However, they should be taught to uphold their teachers, and other adults, with the utmost respect.

A good learning environment should be friendly; discussion oriented, and has discipline. Children need to be challenged to grow and prosper. I can meet this need by using real-life experiences, cooperative groups, best practices, and interactive opportunities in my classroom.

I feel that teachers should be knowledgeable, flexible, and compassionate. Teachers must be able to adapt to the everyday changes in life to create a smooth transition for their students. Knowledge is necessary for any teacher to ensure a quality education for all children. A teacher's compassion can only improve their teaching. Caring for students and their education is an essential ingredient for any effective teacher.

The curriculum has to be aligned throughout the country. Research on aligning curriculum with standards and assessments shows a strong relationship to student achievement (Price-Baugh, 1997;

Mitchell, 1998; Wishnick, 1989). This research digest summarizes the research literature, specifically addressing textbook alignment, instructional alignment, alignment between state standards and enacted curriculum, curriculum alignment through professional development, and findings from international alignment studies. The following definitions from two experts may contribute to understanding this discussion. Curriculum, states Fenwick English (1999), has three components: the written, the taught, and the tested. The taught curriculum consists of two parts: the lesson plans teachers use to plan what they teach and the actual classroom instruction. Webb (1997) defines alignment as "the degree to which expectations [standards] and assessments are in agreement and serve in conjunction with one another to guide the system towards students learning what they are expected to know and do" (p. 4).

The extent to which textbooks are aligned with standards and assessments is important due to the widespread use of textbooks to guide instruction. Early alignment studies showed a lack of alignment between textbooks and standardized tests (Freeman et al., 1980; Goodman, Shannon, Freeman, & Murphy, 1988). Similarly, Floden, Porter, Schmidt, Freeman, and Schwille (1981) found little alignment between the content of district curriculum guides, which address standards, and a district's adopted textbooks. Recently the American Association for the Advancement of Science (AAAS) Project

2061 evaluated middle and high school math and science textbooks for alignment with a series of benchmarks contained in most state standards (Kulm, Roseman, & Treistman, 1999). Of 12 mathematics textbooks, only 4 were rated satisfactory, and only 3 covered more than three benchmark areas. Science textbooks fared no better. Only one science text was given a satisfactory rating, and this text is not widely available (AAAS, 2005). Reading texts exhibit a similar lack of alignment to standards. Goodman and colleagues (1988) analyzed basal readers and found a lack of alignment in several areas, including alignment of basal comprehension instruction and student instructional needs and alignment of basal curriculum and the content of the formative assessments included in the basal readers. Price-Baugh (1997) examined the effects of alignment between texts and student achievement on the Grade 7 Texas Assessment of Academic Skills (TAAS). The study sample included 10,233 students in 35 middle schools in the Houston Independent School District. The textbook content was identified by TAAS descriptors. Price-Braugh then counted the number of skill-level and application-level word problems for each TAAS descriptor and "correlated the amount of practice and explanation in the textbook for 11 target components with the 2 percentage of students correctly answering TAAS problems on those target components" (p. 109). Student achievement was positively correlated with all but one textbook variable. More than 55% of the variance in achievement was explained by the "number of available skill-level practice items in the textbook for each target component" (p. 111); the number of pages devoted to practice problems; and the number of application-level problems included in the text. Thus, the amount of student practice in areas that are tested is strongly related to student achievement.

Cohen and Stover (1981) examined the alignment between instruction and assessments, labeling the process *instructional alignment*. When Cohen (1987) examined four research studies conducted by his doctoral students (Elia, 1986; Fahey, 1986; Koczor, 1984; Tallarico, 1984), he found that when instruction and assessment were aligned during sample lessons, low-and high-aptitude students both scored well. Effect sizes associated with alignment ranged from .91 to 2.74 sigma. According to Cohen, "the critical effect size considered educationally significant had been defined as .70 sigma" (p. 17). Based on these findings, Cohen argues that "the lack of excellence in American schools is not caused by ineffective teaching, but mostly by misaligning what teachers teach, what they intend to teach, and what they assess as having been taught" (p. 18). Wishnick (1989) investigated a mastery learning curriculum to determine how much of the variance in norm-referenced, standardized achievement test scores is explained by the following factors: (1) gender, (2) socioeconomic status (SES), (3) teacher effect, and (4) scores on locally developed criterion-referenced tests (CRT) designed to measure the same skills as the norm-referenced standardized tests (NSRT). Wishnick found that good alignment between CRT (the locally developed tests) and NRST (the standardized tests) accounted for more than 36% of the variance in performance on norm-referenced standardized tests. Altogether, the remaining variables—gender, SES, and teacher effect—accounted for little of the variance in student scores. Moreover, the alignment effect was more powerful for low achievers than for high achievers. Wishnick acknowledges that SES can be a potent factor in school performance, but notes that it loses its impact when the educational model assumes that all students can demonstrate mastery, and when instruction is designed to ensure that students perform well on competency tests. A study by Mitchell (1998) supports Wishnick's conclusion. Mitchell looked at mathematics achievement among 4,000 third graders in a large school district where 55% of the students qualified for free or reduced-price lunch, an indication of poverty. Mitchell examined the effects of curriculum alignment, socioeconomic level, race, gender, and school size. He found that one year after curriculum was aligned to the district's test, students improved 6 NCEs (Normal Curve Equivalent—a scale for averaging student achievement scores), from 49 to 55 on the ITBS standardized test. According to Mitchell, "There was no statistically significant difference in the effect of curriculum alignment after one year of treatment when analyzed by socioeconomic level, race, gender or school size" (p. 96). A study conducted by Wagner and DiBiase (2001) in a college setting suggests that careful work on sequencing and coordinating topics and instruction around science reform themes may be related to increased student achievement. Students in an experimental group experienced a significant increase in the final test scores for the course after attending chemistry lectures that had been aligned with a chemistry laboratory course, while students in a control group exhibited no such increase. Survey data indicate that students in the experimental group believed that the tight connection between the lectures and the lab experiments helped them understand the lectures.

State standards have challenged schools to provide more and higher-level math courses for all students. To investigate the extent to which state standards have led to change at the school level, Porter, Kirst, Osthoff, Smithson, and Schneider (1994) studied six high schools two in large urban districts and four in smaller suburban/rural districts in six states—that "had significantly increased math and science high school graduation requirements in the 1980s." Some critics had voiced concern that requiring more students to take higher-level courses might result in the "watering down" of those courses, but Porter and colleagues reported that this did not appear to have happened. Rather, they found that "the enacted curriculum in high school mathematics and science was not at all in alignment with the curriculum reform toward higherorder thinking and problem-solving for all students" (1994, p. 8). To find out whether the challenge for more and better math courses was related to student achievement, Gamoran, Porter, Smithson, and White (1997) examined the content of instruction in high school math courses and related it to student test scores. They found high positive correlations between end-of-semester teacher surveys of content taught and student achievement gains. Such high correlations (.5), they concluded, indicate a strong alignment between the taught curriculum and the assessment existed.

McGehee and Griffith (2001) designed a professional development process to help school and district staff develops an understanding of the content of the state and/or standardized tests and the implications for instruction, and to reach a consensus on curriculum scope and sequence that aligns with the state tests. The authors reported that after using this process and aligning the curriculum with the tests, a small northeastern Arkansas district increased each of its Stanford Achievement Test 9 percentile rankings for fourth and eighth grades by at least 10 points. In an experimental design study funded by the National Science Foundation in 2000, the Council of Chief State School Officers investigated the effectiveness of a new research-based model for professional development intended to improve the quality of instruction in math and science in five urban districts (Council of Chief State School Officers, 2002). A total of 40 middle schools made up the pool for random selection of treatment and control groups. The Surveys of Enacted Curriculum produced comparable data that could be used to determine the 4 degree of consistency in the curriculum being taught and any source of variation in the enacted curriculum (Blank, 2002, 2004; Porter, 2002). Teachers in the treatment schools received extensive and sustained in-service professional development on using the data (Blank, 2004). As a result of high teacher mobility and other challenges, a full three years of data were collected from only about a fourth of the original 660 participating teachers. Analysis of these data yielded two conclusions: (1) The model did improve quality of instruction, as measured by increasing alignment with state standards, when comparing instruction in treatment schools to control schools; however, the effects were contingent on the level and effectiveness of implementation within the treatment schools. (2) Schools with a high level of participation in the activities showed greater increases in alignment of instructional content with state standards than did other schools. (Blank, 2004, p. 56)

The Trends in International Mathematics and Science Study (TIMSS), formerly known as Third International Mathematics and Science Study, developed a list of math and science content descriptors so that curriculum from various nations could be described, compared, and aligned. The TIMSS study found that the structure (the alignment) and content sequence of a country's curriculum were related to its outcomes when measured by the TIMSS assessments. Schmidt and colleagues (2001) examined the TIMSS data in middle school mathematics and found a "statistically significant relationship" between achievement gain in the subject area and content standards, textbook coverage, teacher coverage, and instructional time. They stated that "the greater coverage of a curriculum topic area—no matter whether manifested as emphasis in content standard, as proportion of textbook space, or as measured by either teacher implementation variable (coverage or instructional time)—is related to larger gains in that same topic area. . . . The curricular priorities of a country—whether reflected by content standards, textbooks, or teacher behavior—are related to the profile of achievement gains across topics for that country." (Schmidt et al., 2001, p. 261)

Further, the researchers observed that the amount of topic coverage in the textbook determined how well students did on the TIMSS test (Schmidt et al., p. 267). The study also found a relationship between time spent on the topic across countries and student achievement:

"Higher percentages of coverage of a typical topic that involved more demanding performance expectations were associated with larger-than-average achievement gains" (p. 303). The study also found that a country's wealth, as measured by Gross National Product, was not strongly related to overall achievement gains in either math or science. This confirms the findings of Wishnick (1989) and Price-Baugh (1997), reported earlier, who found little relationship between SES and student outcome when alignment was controlled. When Schmidt and colleagues (2001) looked at achievement in just the United States and controlled for socioeconomic status and prior achievement in mathematics, they concluded that the more time a teacher spends on a topic, the greater achievement score for that topic. The researchers concluded that "even a small

amount of additional instruction (as little as a week for each) focused on these key 5 topics would predict large increases in learning (around 20 percentage points)" (p. 344). Schmidt and colleagues (2001) concluded that a significant relationship exists between achievement gains and curriculum. And curriculum is something that school districts have control over, even given the existence of state standards and state tests.

Curriculum alignment includes alignment between and among several educations variables, including state standards, state-mandated assessments, resources such as textbooks, content of instruction, and instructional strategies. The studies reported in this review provide strong evidence from scientifically based research that aligning the various components can have positive and significant effects.

Curriculum and have to be updated every five years in order to compete with other develop nations.

Any teacher who is not licensed by the country (national license) and does not have a certificate of civism will be arrested and prosecuted publicly. The National Board for Professional Teaching Standards offers voluntary national certification for teachers in kindergarten through grade twelve. All states recognize national certification and many states and school districts provide special benefits to teachers holding national certification such as higher salaries. Additionally, many states allow nationally certified teachers to carry a license from one state to another. For teachers to acquire a national certificate, teachers must compile a portfolio showing their work in the classroom and pass a written assessment and evaluation of their teaching knowledge. Currently, teachers may become certified in one of seven areas, which are based on the age of the students and, in some cases, subject area. For example, teachers may obtain a certificate for teaching English language arts to early adolescents (ages 11-15), or they may become certified as early childhood generalists. Moreover, any school that is operating without a license will be shut down.

All businesses should be closed on Sundays for the people to give glory to God and his son Jesus Christ and also to spend time with their families, even God had to rest after creating the universe.

And God blessed the seventh day and made it holy, because on it he rested from all the work of creating that he had done.

Everyone should be urged to wear blue pants, blue jackets, and white shirt. In one word a country that needs to prosper needs to have some time of a dress code like the Jews. In order for a government to amass wealth the mass population needs to be taught to stay away from buying all those brand name clothings, and accessories, instead they should be making clothings to sell to other groups who have not been taught correctly and who believe in fantasies and reveries.

The same way we put people in jail when they commit a crime. There should be a system in place to reward great citizenship.

God should be the center of a government or even a country. Prayers should be part of the school curriculum

Marriage counseling and how to be a great husband and wife should be part of the curriculum. There should be real consequences for infidelity, separation, divorce.

A man can have two wives only if the government approves it, depending on income, first marriage etc…) because most men cheat anyway whether they will admit it or not, so the government might as well get some taxes from it. If you are caught cheating or committing adultery you should be charged a fee.

The laws have to be fair, so both parties involved in such act should be charged a fee and will be forced to take classes that help them deal will cheating. After all, cheating, adultery, fornication are vices.

In case of a divorce if granted by the government, the children involve should live with the closest family member or members and both parents have to pay child-support to the caregivers. Since you can't keep a marriage then therefore, the assumption is that you can't take care of children. That would also minimize the divorce rate. Before a married couple wishes to commit adultery he or she would seriously think about the consequences.

Consequences are outcomes – negative or positive - of a person's action. By their nature, they gauge our behavior because we as humans strive for positive outcomes or consequences. When dealing with disciplining your teenager, there are two types of consequences that you'll need to be concerned with: natural and logical. Both of these types can be positive or negative. To help you get a handle of what each type means, I'll define them and give both a positive and negative example.

Old age consists of ages nearing or surpassing the average life span of human beings, and thus the end of the human life cycle. Euphemisms and terms for old people include seniors (American usage), senior citizens (British and American usage) and the elderly. Senior citizens would be taken care of by their own families and the families would get a stipend every month. This would lower cases against hospitals by older patients and their families. Also, senior citizens called "Le Griot" are considered assets to any particular country. They should be encouraged to put their life experiences on audio-books for the new generation to learn from.

(La caste des griots est née puis s'est développée dans un contexte où n'existaient historiquement ni l'écriture (sauf pour les religieux), encore moins la radio et la télévision. Le griot est ainsi considéré comme étant notamment le dépositaire de la tradition orale).

Children should be respected and cherished. After all, they are the future. They should be taught to be citizens of the world. In such republic the jail population will be low because human beings are good until they are changed by society.

Human nature is sacrificed by the demands of the focus on the development of an intellectual culture. Human Nature is in constant conflict with expectations of society. Virtue confers stability and unity upon the human existence because it subordinates the idle speculation to the active needs of the moral life; it induces strength and vigor to the soul; allows for fall expression of man's genius; existence is solid and permanent. The original nature of man is good but corrupted by society. To be good is to exist according to ones intrinsic potentiality of one's nature. Man's egotistic nature prevents him from regaining the simplicity of original human nature. Self love is always good in its purest state and spontaneous; it expresses the real essence of human existence. Self love serves as a source of all genuinely natural impulses and emotions; from instinctively displayed in self preservation to a nobler expression when combined with reason. Natural order affects all aspects of human existence; brings individual into contact with his own inner self, physical environment and his fellow man. All passions are good if they are under our control; all are bad if they control us. Man's nature is not fully mature until it becomes social. Natural man in the state of nature is predominately an instinctive primitive creature living on the spontaneous expression of his innate vitality; man in the social state is a rational, moral being aware of obligations to other people, cafled upon to subordinate the impulse of goodness to the demands of virtue -- a moral and relative existence. Rational man always has an awareness of common good and the need to live in harmonious relationship with his fellow man. Man's ultimate feeling of satisfaction is to feel himself at one with a God created system in which all is good; goal of human endeavor is happiness.

Society should work in alignment with human goodness. Children should be taught to respect their elders, nature, government, country, school, parents, and most of all God.

It's very important to have televised capital punishment to restrict other citizens from committing heinous crimes. Capital punishment, also referred to as the Death penalty, is the judicially ordered execution of a prisoner as a punishment for a serious crime, often called a *capital offence* or a *capital crime.* In those jurisdictions that practice capital punishment, its use is usually restricted to a small number of criminal offences, principally, treason and murder, that is, the *deliberate* premeditated killing of another person. Prisoners who have been sentenced to death are usually kept segregated from other prisoners in a special part of the prison, pending their execution. In some places this segregated area is known as *Death Row*. There are people in this world who are so savage that they can not live in society without reigning terror and murder on their fellow man. I believe the ultimate punishment (death) is well warranted for ultimate crimes- like those of serial killers. To do any less in terms of punishment is to dishonor the victims.

Parents of children born out-of wedlock should have to pay a hefty price to the government and to society. A lot of times when these kids only have one parent, first they became a heavy burden on tax-payers. Second, usually because of the trauma and the lack of parenting these beautiful young people become frustrated, dislike school and they even become suicidal. Remember in every case there are exceptions. Of course some children who are born in a single parent home can become president; this is a chance we would rather not take.

Use of *profanity, dressing indecently, disturbing public peace, unhealthy noise and littering and loitering* would be major offenses.

In order to avoid teacher shortage since everybody in the community is a teacher, parent, a member of the community of some sort. People or community members would be invited to join a school as a visiting educator after several workshops offered by the local school district. Just like jury duty it should be mandatory for community members to be active part of the school in their areas.

Schools should be year-round with two weeks off in December, two weeks in April, and three weeks in July.

All children in spite of class, income should receive free breakfast, lunches, snacks. Parents are responsible for uniforms and their yearly give-back to their parent school-district.

If a student can not do well in school there should other options available to educate that kid, such as, business school, technical school, Army Junior. Everyone without exception should have a minimum education.

All school building across the country should be uniformed under the penal code of the Building Enforcement Agency, which is under Natural Resources and Highways Sub-Council.

In school every student should be required to read ten or more books a year. There should be major exams before going to any grades. However, teachers will have the power to give extra points to deserving students who show effort, respect and dedication. Study by heart should be part of the curriculum. If a student can memorize a whole album in a few days why not make memorization part of the lessons.

There should be a dress code for teachers and school administrators and other staff in the building. These adults have to be role models for the pupils. Also, teachers should be the highest paying professionals since they have to train everybody else.

Once you're ready to start developing a dress code, open the process to as many stakeholders as possible. Bring in teachers and community members. Let them state their preferences and be part of a compromise plan. Develop clear goals and reasonable expectations. Consider a policy that gives teachers and principals discretion in establishing dress interpretation at individual schools according to their classroom needs.

In Harford County, Md., 25 miles northeast of Baltimore, Superintendent Jackie Haas says she wished she had taken some of this advice. Last school year, as her school board developed a more stringent dress code for its 40,000 students, she employed what she thought was common sense and urged board members to add language indicating the district's teachers were role models and should adhere to the same standards as students.

She soon found herself arguing with the teachers union, which perceived her statement as bullying.

THE FUNDAMENTAL FAIR PACT

Even though Haas has agreed to sit down with union representatives to talk about the matter, it has been difficult to get past the hard feelings. The matter remains unresolved.

Any man who mistreats a woman mentally and or physically should be mistreated himself by the court system and the media.

Also abusers should be registered as sex-offenders. Stealing should be a major offense and should be treated accordingly. Moreover, betraying your country and use of terror against the state/citizens are forbidden. Anyone who chooses to otherwise will pay a heavy price and it might even cost them their lives.

The systematic use of violence to achieve political ends is not new – among many other examples, it featured during The Troubles in Ireland before its independence in 1922. In recent decades, it has become a common tactic among a wide variety of groups, from independence movements to the secret services of various countries. ...

- Use of terror, especially the systematic use of terror by the government or other authority against particular persons or groups; a method of opposing a government internally or externally through the use of terror.
- Any act including, but not limited to, the use of force or violence and/or threat thereof of any person or group(s) of persons whether acting alone or on behalf of, or in connection with, any organization(s) or government(s) committed for political, religions, ideological or similar purposes, including the intention to influence any government and/or to put the public or any section of the public in fear.
- "Systematic use of terror, manifesting itself in violence and intimidation. Terrorism has been used by groups wishing to coerce a government in order to achieve political or other objectives, and also by dictatorships or other autocratic governments in order to overcome opposition to their policies." [BFH] Often anti-terrorist mercenaries will only do a job if they have a carte blanche to do whatever they want. ...
- Acts of murder and destruction deliberately directed against civilians or military in non-military situations.
- The systematic use of terror, the deliberate creation and exploitation of fear for bringing about political change
- a violent act in violation of the criminal laws of the United States, which is intended to intimidate or influence the policy of a government.
- Terrorist activities are illegal and involve the use of coercion including the use of force, intended to intimidate or coerce, and committed in support of political or social objectives.
- a psychological strategy of war for gaining political ends by deliberately creating a well-founded climate of fear among the civilian population. Such a strategy may be used by an occupying army on the occupied population. Many terrorist acts, especially against an occupying military or against illegal occupants are acts of war or resistance, and not terrorism.
- The calculated use of violence (or threat of violence) against civilians in order to attain goals that are political or religious or ideological in nature; this is done through intimidation or coercion or instilling fear
- Terrorism is a controversial and subjective term with multiple definitions. One definition means a violent action targeting civilians exclusively. Another definition is the use or threatened use of violence for the purpose of creating fear in order to achieve a political, economic, religious, or ideological goal. ...

The attacks on the World Trade Centre and the Pentagon on September 11 confirmed that terrorism had acquired a new face. Terrorists were now engaged in a campaign of suicide and mass murder on a huge scale. Previously it had been possible to believe that there were limits beyond which even terrorists would not go. After the thousands of deaths on September 11, it was evident that at least one group would stop at nothing.

"Terror is often at its bloodiest when used by dictatorial governments against their own citizens."

Terrorism was not always like this. Its history is as much European as Middle Eastern, and as much secular as religious. Far from being willfully indiscriminate, it was often pointedly discriminate. Yet there are some common threads that can be traced through the history of terrorism. What happened on September 11 was a sinister new twist in an old story of fascination with political violence.

The word 'terrorism' entered into European languages in the wake of the French revolution of 1789. In the early revolutionary years, it was largely by violence that governments in Paris tried to impose their radical new order on a reluctant citizenry. As a result, the first meaning of the word 'terrorism', as recorded by the Académie Française in 1798, was 'system or rule of terror'. This serves as a healthy reminder that terror is often at its bloodiest when used by dictatorial governments against their own citizens.

During the 19th century terrorism underwent a fateful transformation, coming to be associated, as it still is today, with non-governmental groups. One such group - the small band of Russian revolutionaries of 'Narodnaya Volya' (the people's will) in 1878-81 - used the word 'terrorist' proudly. They developed certain ideas that were to become the hallmark of subsequent terrorism in many countries. They believed in the targeted killing of the 'leaders of oppression'; they were convinced that the developing technologies of the age - symbolized by bombs and bullets - enabled them to strike directly and discriminately. Above all, they believed that the Tsarist system against which they were fighting was fundamentally rotten. They propagated what has remained the common terrorist delusion that violent acts would spark off revolution. Their efforts led to the assassination of Tsar Alexander II on 13 March 1881 - but that event failed completely to have the revolutionary effects of which the terrorists had dreamed.

Terrorism continued for many decades to be associated primarily with the assassination of political leaders and heads of state. This was symbolized by the killing of the Austrian Archduke Ferdinand by a 19-year-old Bosnian Serb student, Gavril Princip, in Sarajevo on 28 June 1914. The huge consequences of this event were not the ones that Principle and his fellow members of 'Young Bosnia' had envisaged. Princip could not believe that the assassination had triggered the outbreak of world war in 1914. In general, the extensive practice of assassination in the 20th century seldom had the particular effects for which terrorists hoped.

In the half-century after the World War Two, terrorism broadened well beyond assassination of political leaders and heads of state. In certain European colonies, terrorist movements developed, often with two distinct purposes. The first was obvious: to put pressure on the colonial powers (such as Britain, France, and the Netherlands) to hasten their withdrawal. The second was more subtle: to intimidate the indigenous population into supporting a particular group's claims to leadership of the emerging post-colonial state. Sometimes these strategies had some success, but not always. India's achievement of independence in 1947 was mainly the result, not of terrorism, but of the movement of non-violent civil disobedience led by Gandhi. In Malaya, communist terrorists launched a major campaign in 1948, but they failed due to a mixture of determined British military opposition and a programme of political reform leading to independence.

Terrorism did not end after the winding-up of the main European overseas empires in the 1950s and 1960s. It continued in many regions in response to many circumstances. In South-East Asia, the

Middle East and Latin America there were killings of policemen and local officials, hostage-takings, hijackings of aircraft, and bombings of buildings. In many actions, civilians became targets. In some cases governments became involved in supporting terrorism, almost invariably at arm's length so as to be deniable. The causes espoused by terrorists encompassed not just revolutionary socialism and nationalism, but also in a few cases religious doctrines. Law, even the modest body of rules setting some limits in armed conflict between states, could be ignored in a higher cause.

How did certain terrorist movements come to be associated with indiscriminate killings? When in September 1970 Palestinian terrorists hijacked several large aircraft and blew them up on the ground in Jordan but let the passengers free. Then in September 1972 11 Israelis were murdered in a Palestinian attack on Israeli athletes at the Olympic Games at Munich. This event showed a determination to kill: the revulsion felt in many countries was stronger than two years earlier.

A justification offered by the perpetrators of these and many subsequent terrorist actions in the Middle East was that the Israeli occupation of the West Bank and Gaza (which had begun in 1967) was an exercise of violence against which counter-violence was legitimate. The same was said in connection with the suicide bombings by which Palestinians attacked Israel in 2001-2. In some of the suicide bombings there was a new element, which had not been evident in the Palestinian terrorism of 2 or 3 decades earlier: Islamic religious extremism.

In the 1990s, a new face of terrorism emerged. Osama Bin Laden, son of a successful construction engineer, became leader of a small fanatical Islamic movement called Al-Qaida (The Base). Its public statements were an odd mixture of religious extremism, contempt for existing Arab regimes, hostility to US dominance, and insensitivity to the effects of terrorist actions. Many of its leaders, having helped to free Afghanistan of Soviet occupation in the 1980s, now developed the broader ambition of resisting western dominance, especially in Muslim countries such as Saudi Arabia and Egypt. In pursuit of these ambitions they killed hundreds in bombings of US embassies in Africa in August 1998. Here was a new kind of terrorist movement that had a cause, and a network, that was not confined to any one state, and whose adherents were willing to commit suicide if they could thereby inflict carnage and destruction on their adversaries, as they did on September 11. Since their aims were vague and apocalyptic, there was little scope for any kind of compromise or negotiation.

Can the huge variety of forms of action be categorized under the single label of 'terrorist'? The term is contentious: very few people apart from the Russian Tsar-killers have actually called themselves terrorists. Yet there are some common factors that can be detected behind the many changing faces of terrorism. First, it usually has an unofficial character, claiming to be the result of an upsurge of public feeling. (Of course many governments secretly instigate or support it.) Second, terrorism is based on a naïve belief that a few acts of violence, often against symbolic targets representing the power of the adversary, will transform the political landscape in a beneficial way. Third, terrorism has become increasingly involved in attacking innocent civilians - often with the purpose of demonstrating that the state is incapable of protecting its own people. Fourth, terrorists generally underestimate the strong revulsion of ordinary people to acts of political violence.

There is a further common factor - the tendency of terrorism to become endemic in particular countries and regions. Started by the Left, it has been continued by the Right, and vice versa. Started in a nationalist cause, it is then employed in resistance to the resulting state. Started to cleanse society of corruption and external control, it continues in support of the drug trade and prostitution. If violence becomes a habit, its net effect can be to prevent economic development, to provide a justification for official violence, and to perpetuate existing patterns of dominance and submission.

The facile and oft-repeated statement 'One man's terrorist is another man's freedom fighter' reflects genuine doubts about the term. In the past there have been strong disagreements about whether certain movements were or were not terrorist: for example, the Jewish extremist group Irgun in

Palestine in the 1940s, the Viet Cong in South Vietnam from the late 1950s to the mid-1970s, and the Provisional IRA in Northern Ireland from the late 1960s onwards. Famously, in 1987-8 the UK and US governments labeled the African National Congress of South Africa 'terrorist': a questionable attribution even at the time not because there had been no violence, but because the ANC's use of violence had been discriminate and had constituted only a small part of the ANC's overall strategy.

The new face of terrorism as mass murder is significantly changing such debates. The extremism of the September 11 attacks has led to a strong international reaction. As a result, none of the 189 member states of the UN opposed the USA's right to take military action in Afghanistan after the events of September 11, and none has offered explicit support for Al-Qaida. While there remain numerous concerns about the direction of the US and international moves against terrorism, and it is too early to say that the new face of terrorism is on the retreat, it is not too early to hazard the guess that, by engaging in crimes against humanity, the new face of terrorism may have contributed to its own eventual demise.

The philosophies of Descartes and Kant to the contrary, through the **I think** we reach our own self in the presence of others, and the others are just as real to us as our own self. Thus, the man who becomes aware of himself through the "cogito" also perceives all others, and he perceives them as the condition of his own existence. He realizes that he can not be anything (in the sense that we say that someone is witty or nasty or jealous) unless others recognize it as such. In order to get any truth about myself, I must have contact with another person the other is indispensable to my own existence, as well as to my knowledge about myself. This being so, in discovering my inner being I discover the other person at the same time, like a freedom placed in front of me which thinks and wills only for or against me. Hence, let us at once announce the discovery of a world which we shall call inter-subjectivity; this is the world in which man decides what he is and what others are.

Other things such as: fake hair and nails and wigs should be illegal. The Koreans sell it and they do not use it themselves because they know the truth. It's odd but not so odd at the same time. By now, many people expect to walk into a beauty supply store and see a Korean store owner manning the register. Whether you're in the suburbs of Houston or on MLK Blvd in Anytown, USA, you know what to expect. And yet, walking down a street in a Black neighborhood with Black residents and Black customers buzzing about the retail shops, that image of the few Koreans in the neighborhood only existing behind the cash register of liquor, beauty supply and other retail shops is still perplexing.

But what can explain the seemingly random attraction of Black hair to Korean entrepreneurs? Is it that they love Black hair so much? Was there a plan amongst the first wave of Korean immigrants to hone in on the black hair care industry and dominate the beauty supply store market? From a business perspective, it was no coincidence.

The wig business and the explosion of the wig business in South Korea in the 1960s is instrumental to understanding the Korean ownership of beauty supply stores. According to the book "On My Own: Korean Businesses and Race Relations in America", the rise of the YH Trade wig manufacturing company was significant. Founder Yung Ho Chang, conceived the idea of the company while working as the vice-director of Korean Trade Promotion Corporation in the U.S. Between 1965 and 1978, his company exported $100 million worth of wigs.

The wig business was doing so well, especially amongst African-American consumers that the Korean Wig Merchants pushed to corner the market. "In 1965, the Korean Wig merchants joined together and convinced the Korean government to outlaw the export of raw hair," said Aron Ranen, a filmmaker who has documented the marginalization of African-American entrepreneurs in the hair care industry in the film *black hair* "[This ban] made it so that one can only buy the pre-made wigs and extensions." In other words, Korean hair could only be manufactured in Korea. "Six months later, the United States government created a ban on any wig that contains hair from China," effectively putting South Korea in prime position to exploit the market.

The business structure helped set up many Korean entrepreneurs in the sale of wigs and over the past five decades, wig stores have evolved to become full fledged beauty supply stores where hair for weaves and extensions represent the top selling products. Since then, it's been a chain reaction as one store beget another; family members and employees of one store owner duplicated the business. According to said Dr. Kyeyoung Park, associate professor of anthropology and Asian American Studies at UCLA, competition also played a role in the proliferation. "Korean immigrants are more concerned with peer competition," she said. "If one is running a business so well, then another Korean will open up a similar business very quickly."

Today, there are over 9,000 Korean-owned beauty supply stores serving a billion dollar market for Black hair. Between manufacturing, distributing and selling these hair care products, Korean entrepreneurs appear to control all major components. Ranen was inspired to make his documentary because of what he saw as the injustice of unfair business practices.

"It's really about allowing black manufacturers to get inside the distribution channel," he said. "'I mean, if you ask me, 'what is your vision for the future?'" Well, right away, it's a 100 black-owned stores opening up right next to Korean stores – a boycott until the Korean stores accept at least 20% black-owned manufactured products. Then we are talking about money in the community."

According Ranin, there are only four central distributors serving beauty supply stores in the country and these Korean owned distributors discriminate against Black store owners in order to maintain their monopoly in the market. Ranin interviewed Lucky White, the owner of Kizure Ironworks which specializes in making styling tools like curling irons, for his 2006 documentary. Ms. White claimed that distributors told her that her products were no longer in demand as an excuse to turn away her products in favor of knock-offs produced by Asian companies

> Anyone who uses any of these items is really showing that he or she is not happy with the way that God made you and remember a just country is on God and His words just like Israel. The whole thing is be proud of who you are.

> The monetary system should be based on cash-credit and work. It should be a combination of all three. I found out that Grandma's way to handle money still works. People used to always use cash envelopes to control their monthly spending, but very few do in today's card swiping culture. The envelope system is a key component of the Total Money Makeover plan because it works. Here are a few simple basics for starting a cash envelope system:

1. **Budget each paycheck.** Budget is a dirty word to most people, but you must budget down to the last dime if you're going to successfully implement the envelope system.
2. **Divide and conquer.** Of course, there will be budget items that you cannot include in your envelope system, like bills paid by check or automatic withdraw. However, you can create categories like food, gas, clothing and entertainment.
3. **Fill 'er Up.** After you've categorized your cash expenses, fill each envelope with the money allotted for it in your budget. For example, if you allow $100 for clothing, put $100 in cash in your clothing envelope for the month.
4. **When it's gone, it's gone.** Once you've spent all the money in a given envelope, you're done spending for that category. If you go on a shopping spree and spend the $100 in

your clothing envelope, you can't spend any more on clothes until you budget for that category again. That means no visits to the ATM to withdraw more money!

5. **Don't be tempted.** While debit cards can't get you directly into debt, if used carelessly, they can cause you to over-spend. There's something psychological about spending cash that hurts more than swiping a piece of plastic. If spending cash whenever possible can become a habit, you'll be less likely to over-spend or buy on impulse.

6. **Give it time.** It will take a few months to perfect your envelope system. Don't give up after a month or two if it's not clicking. You'll get the hang of it and see how beneficial the envelope system is as you dump debt, build wealth, and achieve financial peace! See ... simple!

Certainly, some bills may come in at different times of the month, so you'll need to adjust your written game plan to take it one step further. You need to plan the budget based upon your pay periods. Say that you get paid twice a month. If you can write down which bills you plan on paying from each paycheck, you will not be left with a surprise bill. Spend each month's income and each individual paycheck on paper *before* it comes in. I also have no problem with you adding an envelope with money just to have fun with! As long as you and your spouse have agreed on it, you are fine. There should be no lying. Agree on your budget, agree on your fun money, and be open. Fun money can be anything you want it to be. There are no rules on that envelope, unlike money in the "entertainment" envelope that is used specifically for entertainment.

Theatre should be encouraged in country because it would form the taste of its citizens and give them a finesse in behavior and a delicacy of feeling which is very difficult to acquire without its help. UNESCO presented the Road map for Arts Education at the World Conference 2006 in Lisbon and the Seoul Agenda at the next World Conference 2010 in Seoul. Both conferences confirmed the essential role of the Arts in Education to be provided in all UN countries.

On 25-28 November 2010, European members of IDEA – International Drama/Theatre and Education Association - with official representatives from 18 countries were gathered in Athens for their annual meeting. We have written this manifesto, because we have seen evidence in practice and much research has proved, e.g. in European Projects such as DICE and IDEA projects such as D4LC that Drama/Theatre improve our capacity to collaborate, care and create and make learning memorable. However, most politicians are not yet convinced that appropriate initiatives should be undertaken to revive the educational system for the benefit of our children and the future of our world. We have therefore come to the following conclusions, aims and goals, hoping they will be implemented and supported in all countries in Europe:

a) Drama/Theatre is an independent art subject and needs to be taught as a compulsory Subject in the curriculum

b) It needs to be provided over a number of years, as it is a long-term process requiring continuity and progression

c) The appreciation of drama/theatre should be encouraged in every teacher and child for the achievement of high quality education

d) All teachers must also be provided with the skills to enable them to co-operate with drama teachers and theatre professionals in educational settings

e) Development of further partnerships between education, cultural organizations and theatre practitioners is necessary

f) Drama/Theatre should be integrated as methodology into the teaching of other subjects

g) This integration is effective only with specific teaching of the arts at every level

h) Programs for teachers, drama teachers and theatre artists need to be revised to equip teachers and artists with the knowledge and experience necessary to share the responsibility for facilitating learning, and be able to take full advantage of the outcomes of cross-professional cooperation

  i) Educators as well as artists need to encompass insights into the other's fields of expertise – including a mutual interest in pedagogy

ARGUMENTS:

In accordance with Article 27 of the Universal Declaration of Human Rights "Everyone has the right freely to participate in the cultural life of the community, to enjoy the arts and to share in scientific advancement and its benefits".

Also, Article 31 of the Convention of the Rights of the Child states that: "State parties shall respect and promote the right of the child to participate fully in cultural and artistic life and shall encourage the provision of appropriate and equal opportunities for cultural, artistic, recreational and leisure activity".

Although the Rights of the Child and the Declaration of Human Rights are continually violated in various ways, Drama/Theatre in Education has, in all its manifestations, demanded the rights of all children and young people to co-exist creatively, to experience co-operation and collaboration, and also to dream of both the world's transformation as well as their own.

Culture, art in education, art as education, play, games, enjoyment, creativity, team-work and imagination do not always seem to find the fertile ground they need to flourish in a global reality of financial crisis that reduces the value of human beings and many of the benefits we have gained by collective effort through the centuries for a free, just and more humane world.

We, specialist drama teachers, arts practitioners and theatre artists, who work in education, continue to create the unexpected inside and outside the classroom, inside and outside the schools, in every place and space we work with children and young people. The learning process is no longer limited exclusively to schools. New possibilities for our art pedagogy have resulted from the development of partnerships between schools and cultural institutions.

In each of these spaces, it is our love and enthusiasm that pave different paths of learning for all of us; different paths to get to know life and the world around us. We need to walk on these paths based on our minds and hearts, on our bodies as a whole. The person who grows as a whole, in body, mind and heart, becomes someone who can judge reality, stand up against all kinds of criticism and violation of Human Rights and the Rights of the Child. It is this kind of person that Drama/Theatre in Education tries to create and nurture, in order to keep hope for the improvement of our world alive. It is this world that we want to hand over as heritage to the next generations.

This Manifesto is written for the purpose of addressing politicians and stakeholders, in every European country. This shared declaration is signed by associations that are active in the field of theatre and drama in European countries. We consider this step as essential to the recognition of equal opportunities for cultural and artistic activity in education.

Symbolically, I address our declaration from Athens, where the role of the theatre as pedagogy for citizens was born and was communicated, through the centuries, to people all over the world.

One of the worst crimes in society should be dealing drugs. A drug-dealer is someone who is against society and who is out to destroy the mind of his or fellow citizens.

In prison prisoners become the property of the government. So they should be obliged or forced to work for the government eight hours a day and six days a week for a very minimal salary. Everything that a prisoner wants he or she has to work for, whether it is television, working out etc….prison should not be a hangout place where one sleeps, eats, lifts-weight and gets out only to commit more crime. Prison should be a one shot deal.

The prison system should be used as rehabilitation center in order to help inmates go back to serve their communities as loyal, fruitful citizens. Prisons are meant to protect the community, but incarcerating people has minimal effect on the crime rate. Violent offenders are released to make way for nonviolent first time offenders, and most people, if they survive the prison experience, are worse off when they get out. About two-thirds of all inmates released from prisons are rearrested within three years.

Prisons are meant to punish those who have committed a crime, but usually do so with excessive and unintended cruelty. Violence, including sexual assault, is rampant. The unsanitary living conditions, combined with the absence of adequate health and medical care, mean that prison inmates and workers are highly susceptible to life-threatening diseases like AIDS, hepatitis, TB and food poisoning. These problems frustrate inmates and often lead to anger, depression and more violence.

Perhaps more importantly, prisons are also meant to rehabilitate criminals and to keep them from victimizing others in the future. But they rarely succeed at that goal. Meaningful vocational and educational programs are rarely offered. And if they are, prisoners practically have to run an obstacle course in order to get access to or complete the classes.

And yet, despite the failure of our correctional facilities, we're sending more people to them than ever. Over the past two decades, as a result of harsher sentencing laws and the war on drugs, America has experienced one of the largest expansions in its jail, prison and community corrections populations in history. In 2004, according to Department of Justice, approximately 2.1 million people were in jails or prisons, and 4.9 million more were in some form of community corrections (typically probation or parole). That is roughly 3.5% of the adult population. Unsurprisingly, America leads the world in the number of people it incarcerates per capita.

That is why, short of abolishing prisons, which is not as radical as it sounds, we need to examine how correctional facilities in America can be reinvented.

To begin with, the federal government should implement a "No Prisoner Left Behind" program, which requires state correctional departments to insure that all prisoners pass their GED and complete one or more technical training courses. Moreover, university education should be facilitated for any prisoner upon request. We know that most inmates have no marketable skills to rely on when they get out of jail or prison. It is incumbent on the system to ensure that these individuals have at least a high school education.

We can also reduce prison populations by transferring many nonviolent inmates to community corrections programs. Traditionally, this has meant probation or parole. But, more recently, these programs have also come to rely on electronic monitoring devices, house arrest, chemical castration and intensive supervision, all of which have generally proven to keep inmates in check. In December 2003, in order to deal with budget deficits, Kentucky started releasing numerous short-timers (those with less than a year on their sentence) who had been convicted of nonviolent crimes. This action had minimal effect on recidivism rates.

Once the jail and prison populations come down to a manageable size, correctional officers should be encouraged, through educational and salary incentives, to switch from their current roles--in which they basically function like hotel attendants--to becoming true "Rehabilitation Officers," implementing and managing meaningful rehabilitation programs.

Prison systems should be rewarded for their ability to rehabilitate inmates, not for simply preventing inmates from escaping. State corrections departments should be given more money if their released inmates prove to commit fewer crimes.

Of course, it must be understood that some individuals will never be appropriate for release into society. These people must be housed in secure facilities. But jails and prisons should really be reserved only for the most violent criminals.

They should be smaller, too. Large correctional facilities are costly to run, unnecessarily bureaucratic and impersonal. Smaller physical structures go a long way in minimizing the alienation of prisoners and correctional officers alike. The older facilities can be torn down, used as homeless shelters, or as tourist attractions for the public to see the way that we used to do things.

Within the remaining prisons and jails, we need to re-think the way prisoners are housed. Older, more experienced prisoners typically prey on younger prisoners. This leads to both physical and sexual violence. Over time, younger prisoners become socialized to prison life, making it more difficult for them to re-enter society. Violent prisoners who have committed felonies should never be mixed with first time offenders or people convicted of nonviolent crimes. Inmates should not be used as profit gainers for big companies.

> Unions should be as watchdogs to make sure there is equilibrium and fairness in the workplace. Unions should be working for the embetterment of a society even if it is the tough thing to do.

> Parents have to take care and discipline their kids before the police or the law does. If you don't discipline your kids the cops will.

> When the economy is in trouble government should not be firing people instead it should have a spending and a hiring freeze. Also the rich have to help boost the economy by any means necessary.

The rich has to pay higher taxes in order to support the economy. For more than a century it's been generally recognized that the best taxes (admittedly this is an expression reminiscent of "the most pleasant death" or "the funniest *Family Circus* cartoon") are progressive-- that is, proportionate to income.

Lately, however, it's become fashionable to question this. Various Republican leaders have trotted out the idea of a flat tax, meaning a fixed *percentage* of income tax levied on everyone. And in their hearts they may be anxious to emulate Maggie Thatcher's poll tax a single *amount* that everyone must pay. Isn't that more fair? Shouldn't everyone pay the same amount? In a word-- no. It's not more fair; it's appallingly unfair. Why? The rich should pay more taxes, because the rich get more from the government.

Consider defense, for example, which makes up 20% of the budget. Defending the country benefits everyone; but it benefits the rich more, because they have more to defend. It's the same principle as insurance: if you have a bigger house or a fancier car, you pay more to insure it.

Social security payments, which make up another 20% of the budget, are dependent on income-- if you've put more into the system, you get higher payments when you retire.

Investments in the nation's infrastructure-- transportation, education, research & development, energy, police subsidies, the courts, etc…Aagain are more useful the more you have. The interstates and airports benefit interstate commerce and people who can travel, not ghetto dwellers. Energy is used disproportionately by the rich and by industry.

As for public education, the better public schools are the ones attended by the moderately well off. The *very* well off ship their offspring off to private schools; but it is their companies that benefit from a well-educated public. (If you don't think that's a benefit, go start up an engineering firm, or even a factory, in El Salvador. Or Watts.)

The FDIC and the S&L bailout obviously most benefit investors and large depositors. A neat example: a smooth operator bought a failing S&L for $350 million, then received $2 billion from the government to help resurrect it.

Beyond all this, the federal budget is top-heavy with corporate welfare. Counting tax breaks and expenditures, corporations and the rich snuffle up over $400 billion a year compare that to the $1400 budget, or the $116 billion spent on programs for the poor.

Where's all that money go? There's direct subsidies to agribusiness ($18 billion a year), to export companies, to maritime shippers, and to various industries-- airlines, nuclear power companies, timber companies, mining companies, automakers, drug companies. There's billions of dollars in military waste and fraud. And there's untold billions in tax credits, deductions, and loopholes. Accelerated depreciation alone, for instance, is estimated to cost the Treasury $37 billion a year-- billions more than the mortgage interest deduction. (Which itself benefits the people with the biggest mortgages. But we should encourage home ownership, shouldn't we? Well, Canada has no interest deduction, but has about the same rate of home ownership.)

Everyone should have healthcare In the United States (and the world, for that matter), access to healthcare should be a right, just like the right to an attorney if you are charged with a crime. I believe that most people would agree with the goal, but are deathly afraid of what the solution might bring, or that someone might abuse the system and ruin it for the rest of us. regardless of class, economic status, skin color, religious belief and so forth everyone should have access to healthcare.

> A country has to have the right to protect itself from outside enemies. So nuclear power is a good way to bring about this protection.

> As a nation we need to take care of our land. For a state to prosper the government has to truly support agriculture. Take a look at President Truman speech in the state of the Union in 1948. the productive strength of our farms and factories.

More important, however, is the fact that these years brought us new courage, new confidence in the ideals of our free democracy. Our deep belief in freedom and justice was reinforced in the crucible of war.

On the foundations of our greatly strengthened economy and our renewed confidence in democratic values, we can continue to move forward.

There are some who look with fear and distrust upon planning for the future. Yet our great national achievements have been attained by those with vision. Our Union was formed, our frontiers were pushed back, and our great industries were built by men wh o looked ahead.

I propose that we look ahead today toward those goals for the future which have the greatest bearing upon the foundations of our democracy and the happiness of our people.

I do so, confident in the thought that with clear objectives and with firm determination, we can, in the next 10 years, build upon the accomplishments of the past decades to achieve a glorious future.

Year by year, beginning now, we must make a substantial part of this progress. Our first goal is to secure fully the essential human rights of our citizens.

The United States has always had a deep concern for human rights. Religious freedom, free speech, and freedom of thought are cherished realities in our land. Any denial of human rights is a denial of the basic beliefs of democracy and of our regard for the worth of each individual.

Today, however, some of our citizens are still denied equal opportunity for education, for jobs and economic advancement, and for the expression of their views at the polls. Most serious of all, some are denied equal protection under laws. Whether discrimination is based on race, or creed, or color, or land of origin, it is utterly contrary to American ideals of democracy.

The recent report of the President's Committee on Civil Rights points out the way to corrective action by the Federal Government and by State and local governments. Because of the need for effective Federal action, I shall send a special message to the Congress on this important subject.

We should also consider our obligation to assure the fullest possible measure of civil rights to the people of our territories and possessions. I believe that the time has come for Alaska and Hawaii to be admitted to the Union as States. Our second goal is to protect and develop our human resources.

The safeguarding of the rights of our citizens must be accompanied by an equal regard for their opportunities for development and their protection from economic insecurity. In this Nation the ideals of freedom and equality can be given specific meaning in terms of health, education, social security, and housing.

Over the past 12 years we have erected a sound framework of social security legislation. Many millions of our citizens are now protected against the loss of income which can come with unemployment, old age, or the death of wage earners. Yet our system has gaps and inconsistencies; it is only half finished.

We should now extend unemployment compensation, old age benefits, and survivors' benefits to millions who are not now protected. We should also raise the level of benefits.

The greatest gap in our social security structure is the lack of adequate provision for the Nation's health. We are rightly proud of the high standards of medical care we know how to provide in the United States. The fact is, however, that most of our p eople cannot afford to pay for the care they need.

I have often and strongly urged that this condition demands a national health program. The heart of the program must be a national system of payment for medical care based on well-tried insurance principles. This great Nation cannot afford to allow its c itizens to suffer needlessly from the lack of proper medical care.

Our ultimate aim must be a comprehensive insurance system to protect all our people equally against insecurity and ill health. Another fundamental aim of our democracy is to provide an adequate education for every person.

Our educational systems face a financial crisis. It is deplorable that in a Nation as rich as ours there are millions of children who do not have adequate schoolhouses or enough teachers for a good elementary or secondary education. If there are educat ional inadequacies in any State, the whole Nation suffers. The Federal Government has a responsibility for providing financial aid to meet this crisis.

In addition, we must make possible greater equality of opportunity to all our citizens for education. Only by so doing can we insure that our citizens will be capable of understanding and sharing the responsibilities of democracy.

The Government's programs for health, education, and security are of such great importance to our democracy that we should now establish an executive department for their administration.

Health and education have their beginning in the home. No matter what our hospitals or schools are like, the youth of our Nation are handicapped when millions of them live in city slums and country shacks. Within the next decade, we must see that every A merican family has a decent home. As an immediate step we need the long range housing program which I have recommended on many occasions to this Congress. This should include financial aids designed to yield more housing at lower prices. It should provi de public housing for low-income families, and vigorous development of new techniques to lower the cost of building.

Until we can overcome the present drastic housing shortage, we must extend and strengthen rent control.

We have had, and shall continue to have, a special interest in the welfare of our veterans. Over 14 million men and women who served in the armed forces in World War II have now returned to civilian life. Over 2 million veterans are being helped through school. Millions have been aided while finding jobs, and have been helped in buying homes, in obtaining medical care, and in adjusting themselves to physical handicaps.

All but a very few veterans have successfully made the transition from military life to their home communities. The success of our veterans' program is proved by this fact. This Nation is proud of the eagerness shown by our veterans to become self-relian t and self-supporting citizens.

Our third goal is to conserve and use our natural resources so that they can contribute most effectively to the welfare of our people.

The resources given by nature to this country are rich and extensive. The material foundations of our growth and economic development are the bounty of our fields, the wealth of our mines and forests, and the energy of our waters. As a Nation, we are coming to appreciate more each day the close relationship between the conservation of these resources and the preservation of our national strength.

We are doing far less than we know how to do to make use of our resources without destroying them. Both the public and private use of these resources must have the primary objective of maintaining and increasing these basic supports for an expanding fut ure.

We must continue to take specific steps toward this goal. We must vigorously defend our natural wealth against those who would misuse it for selfish gain.

We need accurate and comprehensive knowledge of our mineral resources and must intensify our efforts to develop new supplies and to acquire stockpiles of scarce materials.

We need to protect and restore our land public and private-through combating erosion and rebuilding the fertility of the soil.

We must expand our reclamation program to bring millions of acres of arid land into production, and to improve water supplies for additional millions of acres. This will provide new opportunities for veterans and others, particularly in the West, and ai d in providing a rising living standard for a growing population.

We must protect and restore our forests by sustained-yield forestry and by planting new trees in areas now slashed and barren.

We must continue to erect multiple-purpose dams on our great rivers-not only to reclaim land, but also to prevent floods, to extend our inland waterways and to provide hydroelectric power. This public power must not be monopolized for private gain. Only through well established policies of transmitting power directly to its market and thus encouraging widespread use at low rates can the Federal Government assure the people of their full share of its benefits. Additional power - public and private - i s needed to raise the ceilings now imposed by power shortages on industrial and agricultural development.

We should achieve the wise use of resources through the integrated development of our great river basins. We can learn much from our Tennessee Valley experience. We should no longer delay in applying the lessons of that vast undertaking to our other gre at river basins.

Our fourth goal is to lift the standard of living for all our people by strengthening our economic system and sharing more broadly among our people the goods we produce. The amazing economic progress of the past 10 years points the way for the next 10. Today 14 million more people have jobs than in 1938. Our yearly output of goods and services has increased by two-thirds. The average income of our people, measured in dollars of equal purchasing power, has increased-after taxes-by more than 50 percent. In no other 10 years have farmers, businessmen, and wage earners made such great gains. We may not be able to expand as rapidly in the next decade as in the last, because we are now starting from full employment and very high production. But we can increase our annual output by at least one-third above the present level. We can lift our sta ndard of living to nearly double what it was 10 years ago. If we distribute these gains properly, we can go far toward stamping out poverty in our generation. To do this, agriculture, business, and labor must move forward together.

Permanent farm prosperity and agricultural abundance will be achieved only as our whole economy grows and prospers. The farmer can sell more food at good prices when the incomes of wage earners are high and when there is full employment. Adequate diets for every American family, and the needs of our industries at full production, will absorb a farm output well above our present levels.

Although the average farmer is now better off than ever before, farm families as a whole have only begun to catch up with the standards of living enjoyed in the cities. In 1946, the average income of farm people was $779, contrasted with an average incom e of $1,288 for non-farm people. Within the next decade, we should eliminate elements of inequality in these living standards.

To this end our farm program should enable the farmer to market his varied crops at fair price levels and to improve his standard of living.

We need to continue price supports for major farm commodities on a basis which will afford reasonable protection against fluctuations in the levels of production and demand. The present price support program must be reexamined and modernized.

Crop insurance should be strengthened and its benefits extended in order to protect the farmer against the special hazards to which he is subject.

We also need to improve the means for getting farm products into markets and into the hands of consumers. Cooperatives which directly or indirectly serve this purpose must be encouraged - not discouraged. The school lunch program should be continued and adequately financed.

We need to go forward with the rural electrification program to bring the benefits of electricity to all our farm population.

We can, and must, aid and encourage farmers to conserve their soil resources and restore the fertility of the land that has suffered from neglect or unwise use.

All these are practical measures upon which we should act immediately to enable agriculture to make its full contribution to our prosperity.

We must also strengthen our economic system within the next decade by enlarging our industrial capacity within the framework of our free enterprise system.

We are today far short of the industrial capacity we need for a growing future. At least $50 billion should be invested by industry to improve and expand our productive facilities over the next few years. But this is only the beginning. The industrial application of atomic energy and other scientific advances will constantly open up further opportunities for expansion. Farm prosperity and high employment will call for an immensely increased output of goods and services.

Growth and vitality in our economy depend on vigorous private enterprise. Free competition is the key to industrial development, full production and employment, fair prices, and an ever improving standard of living. Competition is seriously limited tod ay in many industries by the concentration of economic power and other elements of monopoly. The appropriation of sufficient funds to permit proper enforcement of the present antitrust laws is essential. Beyond that we should go on to strengthen our legislation to protect competition. Another basic element of a strong economic system is the well-being of the wage earners.

We have learned that the well-being of workers depends on high production and consequent high employment. We have learned equally well that the welfare of industry and agriculture depends on high incomes for our workers.

The Government has wisely chosen to set a floor under wages. But our 40-cent minimum wage is inadequate and obsolete. I recommend the lifting of the minimum wage to 75 cents an hour.

In general, however, we must continue to rely on our sound system of collective bargaining to set wage scales. Workers' incomes should increase at a rate consistent with the maintenance of sound price, profit, and wage relationships and with increase of productivity.

The Government's part in labor-management relations is now largely controlled by the terms of the Labor-Management Relations Act of 1947. I made my attitude clear on this act in my veto message to the Congress last June. Nothing has occurred since to change my opinion of this law. As long as it remains the law of the land, however, I shall carry out my constitutional duty and administer it.

As we look ahead we can understand the crucial importance of restraint and wisdom in arriving at new labor-management contracts. Work stoppages would result in a loss of production-a loss which could bring higher prices for our citizens and could also d eny the necessities of life to the hard pressed peoples of other lands. It is my sincere hope that the representatives of labor and of industry will bear in mind that the Nation as a whole has a vital stake in the success of their bargaining efforts.

If we surmount our current economic difficulties, we can move ahead to a great increase in our national income which will enable all our people to enjoy richer and fuller lives.

All of us must advance together. One fifth of our families now have average annual incomes of less than $850. We must see that our gains in national income are made more largely available to those with low incomes, whose need is greatest. This will bene fit us all through providing a stable foundation of buying power to maintain prosperity.

Business, labor, agriculture, and Government, working together, must develop the policies which will make possible the realization of the full benefits of our economic system.

Our fifth goal is to achieve world peace based on principles of freedom and justice and the equality of all nations.

Twice within our generation, world wars have taught us that we cannot isolate ourselves from the rest of the world.

We have learned that the loss of freedom in any area of the world means a loss of freedom to ourselves - that the loss of independence by any nation adds directly to the insecurity of the United States and all free nations.

We have learned that a healthy world economy is essential to world peace-that economic distress is a disease whose evil effects spread far beyond the boundaries of the afflicted nation.

For these reasons the United States is vigorously following policies designed to achieve a peaceful and prosperous world.

We are giving, and will continue to give, our full support to the United Nations. While that organization has encountered unforeseen and unwelcome difficulties, I am confident of its ultimate success. We are also devoting our efforts toward world econom ic recovery and the revival of world trade. These actions are closely related and mutually supporting.

We believe that the United States can be an effective force for world peace only if it is strong. We look forward to the day when nations will decrease their armaments. Yet so long as there remains serious opposition to the ideals of a peaceful world, w e must maintain strong armed forces.

The passage of the National Security Act by the Congress at its last session was a notable step in providing for the security of this country. A further step which I consider of even greater importance is the early provision for universal training. There are many elements in a balanced national security program, all interrelated and necessary, but universal training should be the foundation for them all. A favorable decision by the Congress at an early date is of world importance. I am convinced that su ch action is vital to the security of this Nation and to the maintenance of its leadership.

The United States is engaged today in many international activities directed toward the creation of lasting peaceful relationships among nations.

We have been giving substantial aid to Greece and Turkey to assist those nations in preserving their integrity against foreign pressures. Had it not been for our aid, their situation today might well be radically different. The continued integrity of th ose countries will have a powerful effect upon other nations in the Middle East and in Europe struggling to maintain their independence while they repair the damages of war.

The United States has special responsibilities with respect to the countries in which we have occupation forces: Germany, Austria, Japan, and Korea. Our efforts to reach agreements on peace settlements for these countries have so far been blocked. But we shall continue to exert our utmost efforts to obtain satisfactory settlements for each of these nations.

Many thousands of displaced persons, still living in camps overseas, should be allowed entry into the United States. I again urge the Congress to pass suitable legislation at once so that this Nation may do its share in caring for the homeless and suffer ing refugees of all faiths. I believe that the admission of these persons will add to the strength and energy of this Nation.

We are moving toward our goal of world peace in many ways. But the most important efforts which we are now making are those which support world economic reconstruction. We are seeking to restore the world trading system which was shattered by the war an d to remedy the economic paralysis which grips many countries.

To restore world trade we have recently taken the lead in bringing about the greatest reduction of world tariffs that the world has ever seen. The extension of the provisions of the Reciprocal Trade Agreements Act, which made this achievement possible, is of extreme importance. We must also go on to support the International Trade Organization, through which we hope to obtain worldwide agreement on a code of fair conduct in international trade.

Our present major effort toward economic reconstruction is to support the program for recovery developed by the countries of Europe. In my recent message to the Congress, I outlined the reasons why it is wise and necessary for the United States to extend this support.

I want to reaffirm my belief in the soundness and the promise of this proposal. When the European economy is strengthened, the product of its industry will be of benefit to many other areas of economic distress. The ability of free men to overcome hunger and despair will be a moral stimulus to the entire world.

We intend to work also with other nations in achieving world economic recovery. We shall continue our cooperation with the nations of the Western Hemisphere. A special program of assistance to China, to provide urgent relief needs and to speed reconstruction, will be submitted to the Congress.

Unfortunately, not all governments share the hope of the people of the United States that economic reconstruction in many areas of the world can be achieved through cooperative effort among nations. In spite of these differences we will go forward with o ur efforts to overcome economic paralysis.

No nation by itself can carry these programs to success; they depend upon the cooperative and honest efforts of all participating countries. Yet the leadership is inevitably ours.

I consider it of the highest importance that the Congress should authorize support for the European recovery program for the period from April 1, 1948, to June 30, 1952, with an initial amount for the first 15 months of $6.8 billion. I urge the Congress to act promptly on this vital measure of our foreign policy this decisive contribution to world peace.

We are following a sound, constructive, and practical course in carrying out our determination to achieve peace.

We are fighting poverty, hunger, and suffering. This leads to peace-not war. We are building toward a world where all nations, large and small alike, may live free from the fear of aggression.

This leads to peace-not war. Above all else, we are striving to achieve a concord among the peoples of the world based upon the dignity of the individual and the brotherhood of man. This leads to peace-not war.

We can go forward with confidence that we are following sound policies, both at home and with other nations, which will lead us toward our great goals for economic, social and moral achievement.

As we enter the New Year, we must surmount one major problem which affects all our goals. That is the problem of inflation.

Already inflation in this country is undermining the living standards of millions of families. Food costs too much. Housing has reached fantastic price levels. Schools and hospitals are in financial distress. Inflation threatens to bring on disagreem ent and strife between labor and management.

Worst of all, inflation holds the threat of another depression, just as we had a depression after the unstable boom following the First World War.

When I announced last October that the Congress was being called into session, I described the price increases which had taken place since June 1946. Wholesale prices had increased 40 percent; retail prices had increased 23 percent.

Since October prices have continued to rise. Wholesale prices have gone up at an annual rate of 18 percent. Retail prices have gone up at an annual rate of 10 percent.

The events which have occurred since I presented my 10-point anti-inflation program to the Congress in November have made it even clearer that all in points are essential. High prices must not be our means of rationing. We must deal effectively and at once with the high cost of living. We must stop the spiral of inflation.

I trust that within the shortest possible time the Congress will make available to the Government the weapons that are so desperately needed in the fight against inflation.

One of the most powerful anti-inflationary factors in our economy today is the excess of Government revenues over expenditures.

Government expenditures have been and must continue to be held at the lowest safe levels. Since V - J Day Federal expenditures have been sharply reduced. They have been cut from more than $63 billion in the fiscal year 1946 to less than $38 billion in the present fiscal year. The number of civilian employees has been cut nearly in half-from 3/4 million down to 2 million.

On the other hand, Government revenues must not be reduced. Until inflation has been stopped there should be no Cut in taxes that is not offset by additions at another point in our tax structure.

Certain adjustments should be made within our existing tax structure that will not affect total receipts, yet will adjust the tax burden so that those least able to pay will have their burden lessened by the transfer of a portion of it to those best able to pay.

Many of our families today are suffering hardship because of the high cost of living. At the same time profits of corporations have reached an all-time record in 1947. Corporate profits total $17 billion after taxes. This compared with $12.5 billion in 1 946, the previous high year.

Because of this extraordinarily high level of profits, corporations can well afford to carry a larger share of the tax load at this time.

During this period in which the high cost of living is bearing down on so many of our families, tax adjustments should be made to ease their burden. The low-income group particularly is being pressed very hard. To this group a tax adjustment would resul t in a saving that could be used to buy the necessities of life.

I recommend therefore that, effective January I, 1948, a cost of living tax credit be extended to our people consisting of a credit of $40 to each individual taxpayer and an additional credit of $40 for each dependent. Thus the income tax of a man with a wife and two children would be reduced $160. The credit would be extended to all taxpayers, but it would be particular helpful to those in the low-income group.

It is estimated that such a tax credit would reduce Federal revenue by $3.2 billion. This reduction should be made up by increasing the tax on corporate profits in an amount that will produce this sum-with appropriate adjustment for small corporations.

This is the proper method of tax relief at this time. It gives relief to those who need it most without cutting the total tax revenue of the Government.

When the present danger of inflation has passed we should consider tax reduction based upon a revision of our entire tax structure.

When we have conquered inflation, we shall be in a position to move forward toward our chosen goals. As we do so, let us keep ever before us our high purposes.

We are determined that every citizen of this Nation shall have an equal right and an equal opportunity to grow in wisdom and in stature and to take his place in the control of his Nation's destiny.

We are determined that the productive resources of this Nation shall be used wisely and fully for the benefit of all.

We are determined that the democratic faith of our people and the strength of our resources shall contribute their full share to the attainment of enduring peace in the world.

It is our faith in human dignity that underlies these purposes. It is this faith that keeps us a strong and vital people.

This is a time to remind ourselves of these fundamentals. For today the whole world looks to us for leadership. This is the hour to rededicate ourselves to the faith in mankind that makes us strong. This is the hour to rededicate ourselves to the faith in God that gives us confidence as we face the challenge of the years ahead.

Moreover, as species we need to take care of our planets by encouraging recycling, saving water, saving electricity and going green.

> Any other race or ethnic group that declares war against a foreign country, whether it is religious or any kind of war that group of people if there are any living in the target country will be expulsed; naturalized or not, except the natives. *Sometimes tolerance can be equal to death and extinction.*

The child support system in a country should be fair to both mothers and fathers. We should recognize that fathers rights groups have been right all along. Credible research showing that child support awards needed to be increased has never existed. (Nor has it ever been shown that increased enforcement would be beneficial, and it has for the most part not been.) States need to reform their laws in order to meet the federal requirement to assure a just and appropriate child support award in each case. A father should be able to petition the courts for debt relief, just like a mother can ask that a debt be forgiven. The child support system should not be rewarding women for having ex-amount of babies and bringing down the rassots on fathers who make the effort to take care of their children.

Just because someone is born in a country does not make him or her an automatic citizen. I am glad we (the U.S.) will finally get a chance to follow the majority of the other nations' policies regarding child births abroad. Senators Pierce and Kavanagh are correct at proposing this bill. A child born in this country of an illegal alien DOES NOT mean that child is a U.S. citizen. If that was the case, then children born abroad of parents stationed overseas would make them citizens of that host nation (which we all know isn't the case). I just refreshed my memory by reading the 14th admendment of the constitution and no where does it say the parents are constitutionally granted citizenship just because their child is born here.

My opinion: 1. if a child of illegals is born in the U.S., the child becomes a ward of the state and put up adoption and the illegal parents are deported. 2. if the illegal parent(s) want the child, they can take the child and the entire family is deported with a birth certificate stating the child's location of birth but his/her citizenship is still that of the parent(s) native country. Plain & simple.

One way to minimize the problem of children born in this country by illegal aliens is to militarize the U.S. boarder and stop the processing of immigration applications until we (the U.S.) get the situation under control.

Children who are born of immigrant parents and whose parents are illegal should be able to file for citizenship when they are eighteen years of age. If they have any criminal records, such choice will not be available for them unless otherwise. They will be considered the same nationality as their mothers in some cases as their fathers, if they are being by their fathers. Illegal immigrants should pay a special fine every year if this requirement is not met they are subject to be deported automatically without warning. For all the talk about illegal immigration, there is a simple solution: fine the companies that hire illegal immigrants about $5,000 per immigrant, give the CEOs jail time and make the companies pay the cost of deporting those illegals. The federal E-Verify system makes it possible to validate an immigrant's status relatively simply and accurately.

If we punish companies for hiring illegal workers, they will stop hiring illegal workers. If there are no jobs for illegal immigrants, they'll quit entering the country. We won't have to worry about a border fence and we'll save billions on the cost of law enforcement, medical care and education services alone.

THERE WILL BE SOME ADJUSTMENTS.

You may have a hard time getting good food at your favorite restaurant until management realizes it has to pay a lot more for legal workers for kitchen help. It will take months for the labor force to stabilize as management struggles to come to grips with paying a wage that will entice Americans not only to take the jobs, but to keep them. That will run the cost of eating out up substantially and probably reduce the quality of food and service at least in the short run, but it's a small price to pay for secure borders. Likewise, the price of groceries will inflate because farmers and processors will have to pay a lot more to lure Americans into picking tomatoes or eviscerating hogs. I'd expect production to fall and prices to rise — at least until we can replace that American-produced food with imports from China, where laborers make

even less money than our illegal immigrants, or until Americans get used to paying $10 a pound for poultry. There will be some losses of local revenue. Illegal workers pay sales taxes, and some pay Social Security taxes on fraudulent accounts. The goods and services illegal residents buy are part of the economy. But, we should be able to offset that by laying off 20 percent of our law enforcement and a number of educators that will no longer be needed and with savings on health care. Maybe those laid off workers can pick watermelons. Businesses will have to absorb higher costs for maintenance and landscaping. Our native workforce won't do that kind of work for minimum wage.

Fortunately, since there is virtually no construction going on, the loss of illegal labor in the building industry should be of little concern. In fact, the new high cost of building should help restore value to the housing market. There will be other fallout. Some businesses and some farmers will fail, but that's what they get for relying on a porous southern border to supply cheap labor.

We can easily stop most illegal immigration. Soon thereafter we'll see the need to create a mechanism to bring many of those same immigrants back into America to go back to work legally.

I suppose men to have reached the point at which the obstacles in the way of their preservation in the state of nature show their power of resistance to be greater than the resources at the disposal of each individual for his maintenance in that state. That primitive condition can then subsist no longer; and the human race would perish unless it changed its manner of existence.

But as men cannot engender new forces, but only unite and direct existing ones, they have no other means of preserving themselves than the formation, by aggregation, of a sum of forces great enough to overcome the resistance. These they have to bring into play by means of a single motive power, and cause to act in concert.

I mean to inquire if, in the civil order, there can be any sure and legitimate rule of administration, men being taken as they are and laws as they might be. In this inquiry I shall endeavor always to unite what right sanctions with what is prescribed by interest, in order that justice and utility may in no case be divided.

I enter upon my task without proving the importance of the subject. I shall be asked if I am a prince or a legislator, to write on politics. I answer that I am neither, and that is why I do so. If I were a prince or a legislator, I should not waste time in saying what wants doing; I should do it, or hold my peace.

As I was born a citizen of a free State, and a member of the Sovereign, I feel that, however feeble the influence my voice can have on public affairs, the right of voting on them makes it my duty to study them: and I am happy, when I reflect upon governments, to find my inquiries always furnish me with new reasons for loving that of my own country.

MAN is born free; and everywhere he is in chains. One thinks himself the master of others, and still remains a greater slave than they. How did this change come about? I do not know. What can make it legitimate? That question I think I can answer.

If I took into account only force, and the effects derived from it, I should say: "As long as a people is compelled to obey, and obeys, it does well; as soon as it can shake off the yoke, and shakes it off, it does still better; for, regaining its liberty by the same right as took it away, either it is justified in resuming it, or there was no justification for those who took it away." But the social order is a sacred right which is the basis of all other rights. Nevertheless, this right does not come from nature, and must therefore be founded on conventions. Before coming to that, I have to prove what I have just asserted.

The most ancient of all societies, and the only one that is natural, is the family: and even so the children remain attached to the father only so long as they need him for their preservation. As soon as this need ceases, the natural bond is dissolved. The children, released from the obedience they owed to the father, and the father, released from the care he owed his children, return equally to independence. If they remain united, they continue so no longer naturally, but voluntarily; and the family itself is then maintained only by convention.

This common liberty results from the nature of man. His first law is to provide for his own preservation, his first cares are those which he owes to himself; and, as soon as he reaches years of discretion, he is the sole judge of the proper means of preserving himself, and consequently becomes his own master.

The family then may be called the first model of political societies: the ruler corresponds to the father, and the people to the children; and all, being born free and equal, alienate their liberty only for their own advantage. The whole difference is that, in the family, the love of the father for his children repays him for the care he takes of them, while, in the State, the pleasure of commanding takes the place of the love which the chief cannot have for the peoples under him.

Grotius denies that all human power is established in favor of the governed, and quotes slavery as an example. His usual method of reasoning is constantly to establish right by fact. It would be possible to employ a more logical method, but none could be more favorable to tyrants.

It is then, according to Grotius, doubtful whether the human race belongs to a hundred men, or that hundred men to the human race: and, throughout his book, he seems to incline to the former alternative, which is also the view of Hobbes. On this showing, the human species is divided into so many herds of cattle, each with its ruler, who keeps guard over them for the purpose of devouring them.

I have said nothing of King Adam, or Emperor Noah, father of the three great monarchs who shared out the universe, like the children of Saturn, whom some scholars have recognized in them. I trust to getting due thanks for my moderation; for, being a direct descendant of one of these princes, perhaps of the eldest branch, how do I know that a verification of titles might not leave me the legitimate king of the human race? In any case, there can be no doubt that Adam was sovereign of the world, as Robinson Crusoe was of his island, as long as he was its only inhabitant; and this empire had the advantage that the monarch, safe on his throne, had no rebellions, wars, or conspirators to fear.

The strongest is never strong enough to be always the master, unless he transforms strength into right, and obedience into duty. Hence the right of the strongest, which, though to all seeming meant ironically, is really laid down as a fundamental principle. But are we never to have an explanation of this phrase? Force is a physical power, and I fail to see what moral effect it can have. To yield to force is an act of necessity, not of will — at the most, an act of prudence. In what sense can it be a duty?

Suppose for a moment that this so-called "right" exists. I maintain that the sole result is a mass of inexplicable nonsense. For, if force creates right, the effect changes with the cause: every force that is greater than the first succeeds to its right. As soon as it is possible to disobey with impunity, disobedience is legitimate; and, the strongest being always in the right, the only thing that matters is to act so as to become the strongest. But what kind of right is that which perishes when force fails? If we must obey perforce, there is no need to obey because we ought; and if we are not forced to obey, we are under no obligation to do so. Clearly, the word "right" adds nothing to force: in this connection, it means absolutely nothing.

Obey the powers that be. If this means yield to force, it is a good precept, but superfluous: I can answer for its never being violated. All power comes from God, I admit; but so does all sickness:

does that mean that we are forbidden to call in the doctor? A brigand surprises me at the edge of a wood: must I not merely surrender my purse on compulsion; but, even if I could withhold it, am I in conscience bound to give it up? For certainly the pistol he holds is also a power.

Let us then admit that force does not create right, and that we are obliged to obey only legitimate powers. In that case, my original question recurs.

It will be said that the despot assures his subjects civil tranquillity. Granted; but what do they gain, if the wars his ambition brings down upon them, his insatiable avidity, and the vexatious conduct of his ministers press harder on them than their own dissensions would have done? What do they gain, if the very tranquility they enjoy is one of their miseries? Tranquility is found also in dungeons; but is that enough to make them desirable places to live in? The Greeks imprisoned in the cave of the Cyclops lived there very tranquilly, while they were awaiting their turn to be devoured.

To say that a man gives himself gratuitously, is to say what is absurd and inconceivable; such an act is null and illegitimate, from the mere fact that he who does it is out of his mind. To say the same of a whole people is to suppose a people of madmen; and madness creates no right.

Even if each man could alienate himself, he could not alienate his children: they are born men and free; their liberty belongs to them, and no one but they has the right to dispose of it. Before they come to years of discretion, the father can, in their name, lay down conditions for their preservation and well-being, but he cannot give them irrevocably and without conditions: such a gift is contrary to the ends of nature, and exceeds the rights of paternity. It would therefore be necessary, in order to legitimize an arbitrary government, that in every generation the people should be in a position to accept or reject it; but, were this so, the government would be no longer arbitrary.

To renounce liberty is to renounce being a man, to surrender the rights of humanity and even its duties. For him who renounces everything no indemnity is possible. Such a renunciation is incompatible with man's nature; to remove all liberty from his will is to remove all morality from his acts. Finally, it is an empty and contradictory convention that sets up, on the one side, absolute authority, and, on the other, unlimited obedience. Is it not clear that we can be under no obligation to a person from whom we have the right to exact everything? Does not this condition alone, in the absence of equivalence or exchange, in itself involve the nullity of the act? For what right can my slave have against me, when all that he has belongs to me, and, his right being mine, this right of mine against myself is a phrase devoid of meaning?

But it is clear that this supposed right to kill the conquered is by no means deducible from the state of war. Men, from the mere fact that, while they are living in their primitive independence, they have no mutual relations stable enough to constitute either the state of peace or the state of war, cannot be naturally enemies. War is constituted by a relation between things, and not between persons; and, as the state of war cannot arise out of simple personal relations, but only out of real relations, private war, or war of man with man, can exist neither in the state of nature, where there is no constant property, nor in the social state, where everything is under the authority of the laws.

Individual combats, duels and encounters, are acts which cannot constitute a state; while the private wars, authorized by the Establishments of Louis IX, King of France, and suspended by the Peace of God, are abuses of feudalism, in itself an absurd system if ever there was one, and contrary to the principles of natural right and to all good polity.

War then is a relation, not between man and man, but between State and State, and individuals are enemies only accidentally, not as men, nor even as citizens, but as soldiers; not as members of their country, but as its defenders. Finally, each State can have for enemies only other States, and not men; for between things disparate in nature there can be no real relation.

Furthermore, this principle is in conformity with the established rules of all times and the constant practice of all civilized nations. Declarations of war are intimations less to powers than to their subjects. The foreigner, whether king, individual, or people, who robs, kills or detains the subjects, without declaring war on the prince, is not an enemy, but a brigand. Even in real war, a just prince, while laying hands, in the enemy's country, on all that belongs to the public, respects the lives and goods of individuals: he respects rights on which his own are founded. The object of the war being the destruction of the hostile State, the other side has a right to kill its defenders, while they are bearing arms; but as soon as they lay them down and surrender, they cease to be enemies or instruments of the enemy, and become once more merely men, whose life no one has any right to take. Sometimes it is possible to kill the State without killing a single one of its members; and war gives no right which is not necessary to the gaining of its object. These principles are not those of Grotius: they are not based on the authority of poets, but derived from the nature of reality and based on reason.

The right of conquest has no foundation other than the right of the strongest. If war does not give the conqueror the right to massacre the conquered peoples, the right to enslave them cannot be based upon a right which does not exist. No one has a right to kill an enemy except when he cannot make him a slave, and the right to enslave him cannot therefore be derived from the right to kill him. It is accordingly an unfair exchange to make him buy at the price of his liberty his life, over which the victor holds no right. Is it not clear that there is a vicious circle in founding the right of life and death on the right of slavery, and the right of slavery on the right of life and death?

Even if we assume this terrible right to kill everybody, I maintain that a slave made in war, or a conquered people, is under no obligation to a master, except to obey him as far as he is compelled to do so. By taking an equivalent for his life, the victor has not done him a favor; instead of killing him without profit, he has killed him usefully. So far then is he from acquiring over him any authority in addition to that of force that the state of war continues to subsist between them: their mutual relation is the effect of it, and the usage of the right of war does not imply a treaty of peace. A convention has indeed been made; but this convention, so far from destroying the state of war, presupposes its continuance.

So, from whatever aspect we regard the question, the right of slavery is null and void, not only as being illegitimate, but also because it is absurd and meaningless. The words *slave* and *right* contradict each other, and are mutually exclusive. It will always be equally foolish for a man to say to a man or to a people: "I make with you a convention wholly at your expense and wholly to my advantage; I shall keep it as long as I like, and you will keep it as long as I like."

Even if I granted all that I have been refuting, the friends of despotism would be no better off. There will always be a great difference between subduing a multitude and ruling a society. Even if scattered individuals were successively enslaved by one man, however numerous they might be, I still see no more than a master and his slaves, and certainly not a people and its ruler; I see what may be termed an aggregation, but not an association; there is as yet neither public good nor body politic. The man in question, even if he has enslaved half the world, is still only an individual; his interest, apart from that of others, is still a purely private interest. If this same man comes to die, his empire, after him, remains scattered and without unity, as an oak falls and dissolves into a heap of ashes when the fire has consumed it.

Indeed, if there were no prior convention, where, unless the election were unanimous, would be the obligation on the minority to submit to the choice of the majority? How have a hundred men who wish for a master the right to vote on behalf of ten who do not? The law of majority voting is itself something established by convention, and presupposes unanimity, on one occasion at least.

I suppose men to have reached the point at which the obstacles in the way of their preservation in the state of nature show their power of resistance to be greater than the resources at the disposal of each individual for his maintenance in that state. That primitive condition can then subsist no longer; and the human race would perish unless it changed its manner of existence.

But, as men cannot engender new forces, but only unite and direct existing ones, they have no other means of preserving themselves than the formation, by aggregation, of a sum of forces great enough to overcome the resistance. These they have to bring into play by means of a single motive power, and cause to act in concert.

This sum of forces can arise only where several persons come together: but, as the force and liberty of each man are the chief instruments of his self-preservation, how can he pledge them without harming his own interests, and neglecting the care he owes to himself? This difficulty, in its bearing on my present subject, may be stated in the following terms:

"The problem is to find a form of association which will defend and protect with the whole common force the person and goods of each associate, and in which each, while uniting himself with all, may still obey himself alone, and remain as free as before." This is the fundamental problem of which the *Social Contract* provides the solution.

The clauses of this contract are so determined by the nature of the act that the slightest modification would make them vain and ineffective; so that, although they have perhaps never been formally set forth, they are everywhere the same and everywhere tacitly admitted and recognized, until, on the violation of the social compact, each regains his original rights and resumes his natural liberty, while losing the conventional liberty in favor of which he renounced it.

These clauses, properly understood, may be reduced to one — the total alienation of each associate, together with all his rights, to the whole community; for, in the first place, as each gives himself absolutely, the conditions are the same for all; and, this being so, no one has any interest in making them burdensome to others.

Moreover, the alienation being without reserve, the union is as perfect as it can be, and no associate has anything more to demand: for, if the individuals retained certain rights, as there would be no common superior to decide between them and the public, each, being on one point his own judge, would ask to be so on all; the state of nature would thus continue, and the association would necessarily become inoperative or tyrannical.

Finally, each man, in giving himself to all, gives himself to nobody; and as there is no associate over whom he does not acquire the same right as he yields others over himself, he gains an equivalent for everything he loses, and an increase of force for the preservation of what he has. If then we discard from the social compact what is not of its essence, we shall find that it reduces itself to the following terms:

"Each of us puts his person and all his power in common under the supreme direction of the general will, and, in our corporate capacity, we receive each member as an indivisible part of the whole."

At once, in place of the individual personality of each contracting party, this act of association creates a moral and collective body, composed of as many members as the assembly contains votes, and receiving from this act its unity, its common identity, its life and its will. This public person, so formed by the union of all other persons formerly took the name of *city*, and now takes that of *Republic* or *body politic*; it is called by its Members *State* when passive. It is *Sovereign* when active, and *Power* compared with others like itself. Those who are associated in it take collectively the name of *people*, and severally are called *citizens*, as sharing in the sovereign power, and *subjects*, as being under the laws of the State. But these terms are often confused and taken one for another: it is enough to know how to distinguish them when they are being used with precision.

This formula shows us that the act of association comprises a mutual undertaking between the public and the individuals, and that each individual, in making a contract, as we may say, with himself, is bound in a double capacity; as a member of the Sovereign he is bound to the individuals, and as a member of the State to the Sovereign. But the maxim of civil right, that no one is bound by undertakings made to himself, does not apply in this case; for there is a great difference between incurring an obligation to yourself and incurring one to a whole of which you form a part.

Attention must further be called to the fact that public deliberation, while competent to bind all the subjects to the Sovereign, because of the two different capacities in which each of them may be regarded, cannot, for the opposite reason, bind the Sovereign to itself; and that it is consequently against the nature of the body politic for the Sovereign to impose on itself a law which it cannot infringe. Being able to regard itself in only one capacity, it is in the position of an individual who makes a contract with himself; and this makes it clear that there neither is nor can be any kind of fundamental law binding on the body of the people — not even the social contract itself. This does not mean that the body politic cannot enter into undertakings with others, provided the contract is not infringed by them; for in relation to what is external to it, it becomes a simple being, an individual.

But the body politic or the Sovereign, drawing its being wholly from the sanctity of the contract, can never bind itself, even to an outsider, to do anything derogatory to the original act, for instance, to alienate any part of itself, or to submit to another Sovereign. Violation of the act by which it exists would be self-annihilation; and that which is itself nothing can create nothing.

As soon as this multitude is so united in one body, it is impossible to offend against one of the members without attacking the body, and still more to offend against the body without the members resenting it. Duty and interest therefore equally oblige the two contracting parties to give each other help; and the same men should seek to combine, in their double capacity, all the advantages dependent upon that capacity.

Again, the Sovereign, being formed wholly of the individuals who compose it, neither has nor can have any interest contrary to theirs; and consequently the sovereign power need give no guarantee to its subjects, because it is impossible for the body to wish to hurt all its members. We shall also see later on that it cannot hurt any in particular. The Sovereign, merely by virtue of what it is, is always what it should be.

This, however, is not the case with the relation of the subjects to the Sovereign, which, despite the common interest, would have no security that they would fulfill their undertakings, unless it found means to assure itself of their fidelity.

In fact, each individual, as a man, may have a particular will contrary or dissimilar to the general will which he has as a citizen. His particular interest may speak to him quite differently from the common interest: his absolute and naturally independent existence may make him look upon what he owes to the common cause as a gratuitous contribution, the loss of which will do less harm to others than the payment of it is burdensome to himself; and, regarding the moral person which constitutes the State as a *persona ficta*, because not a man, he may wish to enjoy the rights of citizenship without being ready to fulfil the duties of a subject. The continuance of such an injustice could not but prove the undoing of the body politic.

In order then that the social compact may not be an empty formula, it tacitly includes the undertaking, which alone can give force to the rest, that whoever refuses to obey the general will shall be compelled to do so by the whole body. This means nothing less than that he will be forced to be free; for this is the condition which, by giving each citizen to his country, secures him against all personal dependence. In this lies the key to the working of the political machine; this alone legitimizes civil undertakings, which, without it, would be absurd, tyrannical, and liable to the most frightful abuses.

The passage from the state of nature to the civil state produces a very remarkable change in man, by substituting justice for instinct in his conduct, and giving his actions the morality they had formerly lacked. Then only, when the voice of duty takes the place of physical impulses and right of appetite, does man, who so far had considered only himself, find that he is forced to act on different principles, and to consult his reason before listening to his inclinations. Although, in this state, he deprives himself of some advantages which he got from nature, he gains in return others so great, his faculties are so stimulated and developed, his ideas so extended, his feelings so ennobled, and his whole soul so uplifted, that, did not the abuses of this new condition often degrade him below that which he left, he would be bound to bless continually the happy moment which took him from it for ever, and, instead of a stupid and unimaginative animal, made him an intelligent being and a man.

Let me draw up the whole account in terms easily commensurable. What man loses by the social contract is his natural liberty and an unlimited right to everything he tries to get and succeeds in getting; what he gains is civil liberty and the proprietorship of all he possesses. If we are to avoid mistake in weighing one against the other, we must clearly distinguish natural liberty, which is bounded only by the strength of the individual, from civil liberty, which is limited by the general will; and possession, which is merely the effect of force or the right of the first occupier, from property, which can be founded only on a positive title.

We might, over and above all this, add, to what man acquires in the civil state, moral liberty, which alone makes him truly master of himself; for the mere impulse of appetite is slavery, while obedience to a law which we prescribe to ourselves is liberty. But I have already said too much on this head, and the philosophical meaning of the word liberty does not now concern us.

Each member of the community gives himself to it, at the moment of its foundation, just as he is, with all the resources at his command, including the goods he possesses. This act does not make possession, in changing hands, change its nature, and become property in the hands of the Sovereign; but, as the forces of the city are incomparably greater than those of an individual, public possession is also, in fact, stronger and more irrevocable, without being any more legitimate, at any rate from the point of view of foreigners. For the State, in relation to its members, is master of all their goods by the social contract, which, within the State, is the basis of all rights; but, in relation to other powers, it is so only by the right of the first occupier, which it holds from its members.

The right of the first occupier, though more real than the right of the strongest, becomes a real right only when the right of property has already been established. Every man has naturally a right to everything he needs; but the positive act which makes him proprietor of one thing excludes him from everything else. Having his share, he ought to keep to it, and can have no further right against the community. This is why the right of the first occupier, which in the state of nature is so weak, claims the respect of every man in civil society. In this right we are respecting not so much what belongs to another as what does not belong to ourselves.

In general, to establish the right of the first occupier over a plot of ground, the following conditions are necessary: first, the land must not yet be inhabited; secondly, a man must occupy only the amount he needs for his subsistence; and, in the third place, possession must be taken, not by an empty ceremony, but by labour and cultivation, the only sign of proprietorship that should be respected by others, in default of a legal title.

In granting the right of first occupancy to necessity and labour, are we not really stretching it as far as it can go? Is it possible to leave such a right unlimited? Is it to be enough to set foot on a plot of common ground, in order to be able to call yourself at once the master of it? Is it to be enough that a man has the strength to expel others for a moment, in order to establish his right to prevent them from ever returning? How can a man or a people seize an immense territory and keep it from the rest of the world except by a punishable usurpation, since all others are being robbed, by such an act, of the place of habitation and the means of subsistence which nature gave them in common? When Nunez Balboa, standing on the sea-shore, took possession of the South Seas and the whole of South America in the name of the crown of Castile, was that enough to dispossess all their actual inhabitants, and to shut out from them all the princes of the world? On such a showing, these ceremonies are idly multiplied, and the Catholic King need only take possession all at once, from his apartment, of the whole universe, merely making a subsequent reservation about what was already in the possession of other princes.

We can imagine how the lands of individuals, where they were contiguous and came to be united, became the public territory, and how the right of Sovereignty, extending from the subjects over the lands they held, became at once real and personal. The possessors were thus made more dependent, and the forces at their command used to guarantee their fidelity. The advantage of this does not seem to have been felt by ancient monarchs, who called themselves Kings of the Persians, Scythians, or Macedonians, and seemed to regard themselves more as rulers of men than as masters of a country. Those of the present day more cleverly call themselves Kings of France, Spain, England, etc.: thus holding the land, they are quite confident of holding the inhabitants.

The peculiar fact about this alienation is that, in taking over the goods of individuals, the community, so far from despoiling them, only assures them legitimate possession, and changes usurpation into a true right and enjoyment into proprietorship. Thus the possessors, being regarded as depositaries of the public good, and having their rights respected by all the members of the State and maintained against foreign aggression by all its forces, have, by a cession which benefits both the public and still more themselves, acquired, so to speak, all that they gave up. This paradox may easily be explained by the distinction between the rights which the Sovereign and the proprietor have over the same estate, as we shall see later on.

It may also happen that men begin to unite one with another before they possess anything, and that, subsequently occupying a tract of country which is enough for all; they enjoy it in common, or share it out among themselves, either equally or according to a scale fixed by the Sovereign. However the acquisition be made, the right which each individual has to his own estate is always subordinate to the right which the community has over all: without this, there would be neither stability in the social tie, nor real force in the exercise of Sovereignty.

I shall end this chapter and this book by remarking on a fact on which the whole social system should rest: i.e., that, instead of destroying natural inequality, the fundamental compact substitutes, for such physical inequality as nature may have set up between men, an equality that is moral and legitimate, and that men, who may be unequal in strength or intelligence, become every one equal by convention and legal right

1. "Learned inquiries into public right are often only the history of past abuses; and troubling to study them too deeply is a profitless infatuation" (*Essay on the Interests of France in Relation to its Neighbors,* by the Marquis d'Argenson). This is exactly what Grotius has done.

2. See a short treatise of Plutarch's entitled *That Animals Reason.*

3. The Romans, who understood and respected the right of war more than any other nation on earth, carried their scruples on this head so far that a citizen was not allowed to serve as a volunteer without engaging himself expressly against the enemy, and against such and such an enemy by name. A legion in which the younger Cato was seeing his first service under Popilius having been reconstructed, the elder Cato wrote to Popilius that, if he wished his son to continue serving under him, he must administer to him a new military oath, because, the first having been annulled, he was no longer able to bear arms against the enemy. The same Cato wrote to his son telling him to take great care not to go into battle before taking this new oath. I know that the siege of Clusium and other isolated events can be quoted against me; but I am citing laws and customs. The Romans are the people that least often transgressed its laws; and no other people have had such good ones.

4. The real meaning of this word has been almost wholly lost in modern times; most people mistake a town for a city, and a townsman for a citizen. They do not know that houses make a town,

but citizens a city. The same mistake long ago cost the Carthaginians dear. I have never read of the title of citizens being given to the subjects of any prince, not even the ancient Macedonians or the English of to-day, though they are nearer liberty than any one else. The French alone everywhere familiarly adopted the name of citizens, because, as can be seen from their dictionaries, they have no idea of its meaning; otherwise they would be guilty in usurping it, of the crime of *lèse-majesté*: among them, the name expresses a virtue, and not a right. When Bodin spoke of our citizens and townsmen, he fell into a bad blunder in taking the one class for the other. M. d'Alembert has avoided the error, and, in his article on Geneva, has clearly distinguished the four orders of men (or even five, counting mere foreigners) who dwell in our town, of which two only compose the Republic. No other French writer, to my knowledge, has understood the real meaning of the word citizen.

5. Under bad governments, this equality is only apparent and illusory: it serves only to-keep the pauper in his poverty and the rich man in the position he has usurped. In fact, laws are always of use to those who possess and harmful to those who have nothing: from which it follows that the social state is advantageous to men only when all have something and none too much.

Every government must work out for itself what is good and right, and no government can escape the obligation of examining itself.

Thousands of years after great religious teachers and philosophers laid out principles for a good life, we still have violence, injustice, wars and blatant greed rampant in human society.

People have a sense of right and wrong. Healthy, well educated people strive to do what is right.

There is a God. The Universe has a purpose. Each person has free will. Each person is responsible for their own decisions. There is Right and Wrong. Life is a learning experience. Any religion which does not respect the rights of non-believers is fundamentally flawed.

Power is derived from physical force, knowledge and money. Individuals and organizations may use their power for socially good or bad purposes. It is the responsibility of government and each of us to ensure that power is properly used.

Capitalism, Communism and Socialism have been tried and found wanting as Just Economic systems. Communism and Socialism lose out to Capitalism for efficiency. Capitalism is an efficient producer of goods and services; but, left unchecked, results in a socially unacceptable distribution of winners and losers.

The function of the local economy is to distribute the goods and services desired by local people in an efficient manner proportional to the effort exerted by the population.

The Global Economy provides an opportunity to achieve improved human productivity. But social processes must be put in place to ensure benefits are shared fairly. The Capitalist economy reacts too slowly to achieve a fair distribution of benefits.

Unrestricted free trade will deliver the most efficient production of goods and services for the entire world economy if the local economies provide a fair distribution of the benefits of that efficiency.

A good government is one whose rulers seek the welfare of the people, whereas a corrupt government is one whose rulers are primarily interested in selfish ends. A good government may therefore degenerate into a corrupt one if the rulers begin to devote themselves to private gain instead of public welfare.

The entire U.S. political system is disingenuous! We need to differentiate between a tax and a social insurance program. Everyone benefits from insurance which reduces the risk of future adverse events. Government mandated social insurance should not be spoken of as a tax. Health insurance and social security should be setup and administrated as insurance systems, mandated by law and administered under contract by public owned corporations. Government in the United States operates on a local, state and federal level.

The world government needs to establish a uniform set of standards in which the various country governments can carry out the will of citizens of each country.

- Social Problems

In achieving various goals, problems can be identified which need to be solved in order to achieve the goal. If we really understand the problem, the answer will come out of it, because the answer is not separate from the problem. Humans have established laws to protect individuals and to protect society.

How do we reach consensus on how much government the people need and how to pay for that government? Surely an educated people can make this determination in a rational manner without needless partisanship.

Perhaps we can put government on a more business like footing. Let's relate a tax paid to a service received and let the people determine how much tax makes sense for any given service at the federal, state and local level.

Social insurance programs would be mandated by law and administered under contract by public owned corporations.

Implicit in everything we do is a set of assumptions. To better understand why we make decisions, we need to state the assumptions in effect at the time the decision is made. Therefore, we need to keep track of the currently active assumptions.

Rule of Law. Individual responsibility. No lying, No cheating, No stealing.

Plans

For each goal we will develop a plan to achieve that goal. We will then add to a general list of plans in order to develop a resource list needed to achieve our goals to help determine the priorities.

Provide for the Rule of Law. To ensure fairness in human dealings, we shall establish a published set of rules for the conduct of our affairs. Society will ensure that the rules are modified as required to ensure fairness and enforced to maximize safety for both the individual and society as a whole.

Ensure that everyone has a meaningful Job. Since there is an abundance of work to perform, there is no need to be inefficient in any job. We should all strive to find ways to eliminate unnecessary work. In the end, this will ensure that everyone achieves maximum benefit from human progress.

RECOMMENDATIONS

- Separate the government's role of establishing and enforcing the Law from the role of running social programs. We need to differentiate between a tax and a social insurance program. Government mandated social insurance should not be spoken of as a tax.
- Social insurance programs would be mandated by law and administered under contract by public owned corporations.
1. Social Security is a retirement system
2. Medicare is a health insurance system
3. Universal health care can be funded by requiring all income earners to purchase health insurance at a fixed percentage of their income without regard to their history or need. Good health care should be a benefit of membership in society.
- Guarantee employment for everyone who wants a job:
1. Eliminate all welfare payments over a brief time interval; say five years. The welfare experiment was a total failure.
2. Eliminate the minimum wage. Let the labor market establish the value of work.
3. Make the state an employer of last resort to ensure that anyone who wants a job receives one. These jobs will serve community needs and be paid from the income tax. The wage rate will be one half of the established poverty level. Jobs of last resort will require a minimum of forty hours per week of attendance on the job.
4. Adjust the number of hours in a work week inversely to the number of jobs of last resort provided by the state
- Relate each tax to a specific function. Remove all non-specific taxes.

TAX COLLECTION

income tax	national defense	federal level
	education	state level
	full employment	state level
property tax	fire and police protection	local level
sales tax	essential government services	state level
	social services	state level
inflation tax	economic stability	federal level
	rainy day funds	state level
sin tax	restoration	state level
	ex. cigarettes - health care	
service fee	specific government service	local/state level
	drivers license, ID	state level
	water, trash, sewage, etc.	local level
fuel tax	roads, highway system	state/federal level

Cohen and Stover (1981) examined the alignment between instruction and assessments,

labeling the process *instructional alignment*. When Cohen (1987) examined for researches studies conducted by his doctoral students (Elia, 1986; Fahey, 1986; Koczor, 1984; Tallarico, 1984), he found that when instruction and assessment were aligned during sample lessons, lowand high-aptitude students both scored well. Effect sizes associated with alignment ranged from .91 to 2.74 sigma. According to Cohen, "the critical effect size considered educationally significant had been defined as .70 sigma" (p. 17). Based on these findings, Cohen argues that "the lack of excellence in American schools is not caused by ineffective teaching, but mostly by misaligning what teachers teach, what they intend to teach, and what they assess as having been taught" (p. 18).

Wishnick (1989) investigated a mastery learning curriculum to determine how much of

The variance in norm-referenced, standardized achievement test scores is explained by the following factors: (1) gender, (2) socioeconomic status (SES), (3) teacher effect, and (4) scores on locally developed criterion-referenced tests (CRT) designed to measure the same skills as the norm-referenced standardized tests (NSRT). Wishnick found that good alignment between CRT (the locally developed tests) and NRST (the standardized tests) accounted for more than 36% of the variance in performance on norm-referenced standardized tests. Altogether, the remaining variables—gender, SES, and teacher effect—accounted for little of the variance in student scores. Moreover, the alignment effect was more powerful for low achievers than for high achievers. Wishnick acknowledges that SES can be a potent factor in school performance,

but notes that it loses its impact when the educational model assumes that all students can

demonstrate mastery, and when instruction is designed to ensure that students perform well on competency tests.

A study by Mitchell (1998) supports Wishnick's conclusion. Mitchell looked at

mathematics achievement among 4,000 third graders in a large school district where 55% of the students qualified for free or reduced-price lunch, an indication of poverty. Mitchell examined the effects of curriculum alignment, socioeconomic level, race, gender, and school size. He found that one year after curriculum was aligned to the district's test, students improved 6 NCEs (Normal Curve Equivalent—a scale for averaging student achievement scores), from 49 to 55 on the ITBS standardized test. According to Mitchell, "There was no statistically significant difference in the effect of curriculum alignment after one year of treatment when analyzed by socioeconomic level, race, and gender or school size" (p. 96).

A study conducted by Wagner and DiBiase (2001) in a college setting suggests that careful work on sequencing and coordinating topics and instruction around science reform themes may be related to increased student achievement. Students in an experimental group experienced a significant increase in the final test scores for the course after attending chemistry lectures that had been aligned with a chemistry laboratory course, while students in a control group exhibited no such increase. Survey data indicate that students in the experimental group believed that the tight connection between the lectures and the lab experiments helped them understand the lectures.

State standards have challenged schools to provide more and higher-level math courses for all students. To investigate the extent to which state standards have led to change at the school level, Porter, Kirst, Osthoff, Smithson, and Schneider (1994) studied six high schools two in large urban districts and four in smaller suburban/rural districts in six states—that "had significantly increased math and science high school graduation requirements in the 1980s."

Some critics had voiced concern that requiring more students to take higher-level courses might result in the "watering down" of those courses, but Porter and colleagues reported that this did not appear to have happened. Rather, they found that "the enacted curriculum in high school mathematics and science was not at all in alignment with the curriculum reform toward higher order thinking and problem-solving for all students" (1994, p. 8).

To find out whether the challenge for more and better math courses was related to

student achievement, Gamoran, Porter, Smithson, and White (1997) examined the content of instruction in high school math courses and related it to student test scores. They found high positive correlations between end-of-semester teacher surveys of content taught and student achievement gains. Such high correlations (.5), they concluded, indicate a strong alignment between the taught curriculum and the assessment existed.

McGehee and Griffith (2001) designed a professional development process to help school and district staffs develop an understanding of the content of the state and/or standardized tests and the implications for instruction, and to reach a consensus on curriculum scope and sequence that aligns with the state tests. The authors reported that after using this process and aligning the curriculum with the tests, a small northeastern Arkansas district increased each of its Stanford Achievement Test 9 percentile rankings for fourth and eighth grades by at least 10 points.

In an experimental design study funded by the National Science Foundation in 2000, the Council of Chief State School Officers investigated the effectiveness of a new research-based model for professional development intended to improve the quality of instruction in math and science in five urban districts (Council of Chief State School Officers, 2002). A total of 40 middle schools made up the pool for random selection of treatment and control groups. The Surveys of Enacted Curriculum produced comparable data that could be used to determine the 4 degree of consistency in the curriculum being taught and any source of variation in the enacted curriculum (Blank, 2002, 2004; Porter, 2002). Teachers in the treatment schools received extensive and sustained in-service professional development on using the data (Blank, 2004).

As a result of high teacher mobility and other challenges, a full three years of data were collected from only about a fourth of the original 660 participating teachers. Analysis of these data yielded two conclusions: (1) The model did improve quality of instruction, as measured by increasing alignment with state standards, when comparing instruction in treatment schools to control schools; however, the effects were contingent on the level and effectiveness of implementation within the treatment schools. (2) Schools with a high level of participation in the activities showed greater increases in alignment of instructional content with state standards than did other schools. (Blank, 2004, p. 56)

The Trends in International Mathematics and Science Study (TIMSS), formerly known as Third International Mathematics and Science Study, developed a list of math and science content descriptors so that curriculum from various nations could be described, compared, and aligned. The TIMSS study found that the structure (the alignment) and content sequence of a country's curriculum were related to its outcomes when measured by the TIMSS assessments. Schmidt and colleagues (2001) examined the TIMSS data in middle school mathematics and found a "statistically significant relationship" between achievement gain in the subject area and content standards, textbook coverage, teacher coverage, and instructional time. They stated

"the greater coverage of a curriculum topic area—no matter whether manifested as

emphasis in content standard, as proportion of textbook space, or as measured by either teacher implementation variable (coverage or instructional time)—is related to larger gains in that same topic area. . . . The curricular priorities of a country—whether reflected by content standards, textbooks, or teacher behavior—are related to the profile of achievement gains across topics for that country." (Schmidt et al., 2001, p. 261)

Further, the researchers observed that the amount of topic coverage in the textbook determined how well students did on the TIMSS test (Schmidt et al., p. 267). The study also found a relationship between time spent on the topic across countries and student achievement: "Higher percentages of coverage of a typical topic that involved more demanding performance expectations were associated with larger-than-average achievement gains"

The study also found that a country's wealth, as measured by Gross National Product, was not strongly related to overall achievement gains in either math or science. This confirms the findings of Wishnick (1989) and Price-Baugh (1997), reported earlier, who found little relationship between SES and student outcome when alignment was controlled.

When Schmidt and colleagues (2001) looked at achievement in just the United
States and controlled for socioeconomic status and prior achievement in mathematics.
They concluded that the more time a teacher spends on a topic, the greater
Achievement scores for that topic. The researchers concluded that "even a small
Amount of additional instruction (as little as a week for each) focused on these key
topics would predict large increases in learning (around 20 percentage points)" (p.
344). Schmidt and colleagues (2001) concluded that a significant relationship exists between achievement and curriculum. And curriculum is something that School
Districts have control over, even given the existence of state standards and state tests.
Curriculum alignment includes alignment between and among several educations
Variables, including state standards, state-mandated assessments, resources such as textbooks, content of instruction, and instructional strategies. The studies reported in this review provide strong evidence from scientifically based research that aligning the various components can have positive and significant effects.

This research digest is based on *The Relationship Between Aligned Curriculum and Student Achievement,* an unpublished literature review completed by David A. Squires
for Edvantia in December 2005.

References

American Association for the Advancement of Science. (2005). *High school biology textbooks: A benchmarks-based evaluation.* Washington, DC: Author. Retrieved December 2, 2005, from http://www.project2061.org/publications/textbook/hsbio/report/default.htm

Blank, R. K. (2002). Using surveys of enacted curriculum to advance evaluation of instruction in relation to standards. *Peabody Journal of Education, 77*(4), 86-120.

Blank, R. K. (2004). *Data on enacted curriculum study: Summary of findings. Experimental design study of effectiveness of DEC professional development model in urban middle schools.* Washington, DC: Council of Chief State School Officers.

Cohen, S. A. (1987). Instructional alignment: Searching for a magic bullet. *Educational Researcher, 16*(8), 16-19.

Cohen, S. A., & Stover, G. (1981). Effects of teaching sixth grade students to modify format variables of math word problems. *Reading Research Quarterly, 16*(2), 175-200.

Council of Chief State School Officers. (2002). *Using data on enacted curriculum—A guide for professional development.* Washington, DC: Author. Retrieved December 2, 2005, from http://seconline.wceruw.org/Reference/PDguideIntro.pdf

Elia, J. S. I. (1986). An alignment experiment in vocabulary instruction: Varying instructional practice and test item formats to measure transfer with low SES fourth graders.

6

(Doctoral Dissertation, University of San Francisco). *Dissertation Abstracts International,* 48-01A:0082.

English, F. W. (1999). *Deciding what to teach and test: Developing, aligning, and auditing the curriculum (Millenium ed).* Thousand Oaks, CA: Sage Publications.

Fahey, P. A. (1986). Learning transfer in main ideas instruction: Effects of instructional alignment and aptitude on main idea test scores. (Doctoral Dissertation, University of San Francisco). *Dissertation Abstracts International,* 48-03A:0550.

Floden, R. E., Porter, A. C., Schmidt, W. H., Freeman, D. J., & Schwille, J. R. (1981). Responses to curriculum pressures: A policy-capturing study of teacher decisions about content. *Journal of Educational Psychology, 73*(2), 129-141.

Freeman, D., Kuhs, T., Porter, A., Knappen, L., Floden, R., Schmidt, W., et al. (1980). *The fourth grade mathematics curriculum as inferred from textbooks and tests.* East Lansing: Michigan State University, Institute for Research on Teaching.

Gamoran, A., Porter, A. C., Smithson, J., & White, P. A. (1997). Upgrading high school mathematics instruction: Improving learning opportunities for low-achieving, lowincome youth. *Educational Evaluation and Policy Analysis, 19*(4), 325-338.

Goodman, K. S., Shannon, P., Freeman, Y. S., & Murphy, S. (1988). *Report card on basal readers.* Katonah, NY: Richard C. Owen.

Koczor, M. L. (1984). Effects of varying degrees of instructional alignment in post treatment tests on mastery learning tasks of fourth-grade children. (Doctoral Dissertation, University of San Francisco). *Dissertation Abstracts International, 46-05A:1179.*

Kulm, G., Roseman, J., & Treistman, M. (1999). A benchmarks-based approach to textbook evaluation. *Science Books & Films, 35*(4), 147-153.

McGehee, J. J., & Griffith, L. K. (2001). Large-scale assessments combined with curriculum alignment: Agents of change. *Theory into Practice, 40*(2), 137-144.

Mitchell, F. M. (1998). *The effects of curriculum alignment on the mathematics achievement of third-grade students as measured by the Iowa Test of Basic Skills: Implications for educational administrators.* Unpublished doctoral dissertation, Clark University, Atlanta, GA.

No Child Left Behind Act of 2001, Pub. L. No. 107-110. (2002).

Porter, A. C. (2002). Measuring content of instruction: Uses in research and practice. *Educational Researcher, 31*(7), 3-14.

7

Porter, A. C., Kirst, M. W., Osthoff, E., Smithson, J. L., & Schneider, S. A. (1994). *Reform of high school mathematics and science and opportunity to learn.* Consortium for Policy Research in Education Policy Briefs. New Brunswick, NJ: Rutgers University, Consortium for Policy Research in Education.

Price-Baugh, R. (1997). Correlation of textbook alignment with student achievement scores. *Dissertation Abstracts International, 58-05A,* 1529.

Schmidt, W. H., McKnight, C. C., Houang, R. T., Wang, H. C., Wiley, D. E., Cogan, L. S., et al. (2001). *Why schools matter: A cross-national comparison of curriculum and learning.* San Francisco: Jossey-Bass.

Tallarico, I. (1984). Effects of ecological factors on elementary school student performance on norm referenced standardized tests: Nonreading behaviors. (Doctoral Dissertation, University of San Francisco). *Dissertation Abstracts International, 45-12A:3623.*

Trends in International Mathematics and Science Study (TIMSS). (2003). Amsterdam: International Association for the Evaluation of Educational Achievement.

Wagner, E. P., & DiBiase, W. J. (2001, September). Development and evaluation of a standards-based approach to instruction in general chemistry. Charlotte: University of North Carolina. *Electronic Journal of Science Education, 6*(1). Retrieved December 5, 2005, from http://www.unr.edu/homepage/crowther/ejse/wagnerdibiase.pdf

Webb, N. L. (1997, January). Determining alignment of expectations and assessments in mathematics and science education. *NISE Brief, 1*(2). Madison: University of Wisconsin, National Institute for Science Education.

Wishnick, K. T. (1989). Relative effects on achievement scores of SES, gender, teacher effect and instructional alignment: A study of alignment's power in mastery learning. Doctoral Dissertation, University of San Francisco. *Dissertation Abstracts International,* 51

BIBLIOGRAPHY

ARSENE, V. Pierre-Noel : Nomendature polyglotte des plantes haïtiennes et tropicales, 1971, Presse Nationale, Port-au-Prince.
BIBLE DE JERUSALEM: Paris, Editions du Cerf, 1955.
MAXIMILIEN, Louis : Le Vodou haïtien, Port-au-Prince, Imprimerie de l'Etat, 1945.
METRAUX, Alfred: Le Vaudou haïtien, Paris, Gallimard, 1958, 6eme EDITION
NOUVEAU LAROUSSE UNIVERSEL: Paris, Librairie Larousse
PRICE-MARS, Jean : Ainsi parla l'oncle, New York para psychologie fondation, 1954.
RITUEL LATIN-FRANCAIS : Maison Mame, Novembre 1947
ROMAIN, J. B. : Introduction au vodou haïtien Port-au-Prince, Revue Conjonction, No. 1, 1970.
TIMOLEON, C. Brutus et A.V. Pierre-Noel : Les plantes et les légumes d'Haïti qui guérissent, 1960. Imprimerie de l'Etat, Port-au-Prince.
Reviewed by D'Arcy Lyness, PhD. Date reviewed: Feb 2004

David Little- Director of the U.S institute of peace's project on intolerance and senior scholar in religion, ethics, and human rights -1997- United States Institute of Peace

Discrimination Attorney.com

David Greenberg- 1997 ed. Of the successful, a California magazine for accountants.

Josh Levy, cavalier Daily opinion columnist

The association for the preservation of Virginia antiquities, Richmond, VA 23220 (Feb 2000)

Robert MC Colley in Dictionary of Afro American slavery, edited by Randall M. Miller and John David Smith, Greenwood Press, 1998 pp 281

Gene Barios, tobacco BBS: tobacco news

The concise Columbia encyclopedia, 1995 by Columbia University press from MS bookshelf.

Immigration," Microsoft Encarta 98 encyclopedia. Microsoft Corporation".

Patrick Minges, beneath the underdog: race, religi9on and the "Trials of tears".

Ten myths, half-truths and misunderstandings about black history, ethnic news watch soft line information, Inc., Stanford, CT (1981)

Studies in the world history of slavery, abolition and emancipation II, 1 1997

Early uses of Indian tobacco in California, California natural history guide: 10 early uses of California plants, by Edward K. Balls, University of California Press, copyright 1962 by the Regents of the University of California ISBN:0-520-00072-2

Whitefield, Theodore Marshall. Slavery agitation in Virginia, 1829-1832. NY: Negro Universities press, 1930 securing the leg irons: restrictions of legal rights for slaves in Virginia and Maryland, 1625-1791

American feminist political scientist Kirsten Amundsen "silent majority: women and American democracy" (1971).

The changing faces of terrorism- professor Adam Roberts < published 8-27-2002>

Terrorism and International order by Lawrence Freedman at al. (Routledge and Kegan Paul for the royal institute of international affairs, 1986).

The terrorists: from Tsarist Russia to the O.A.S by Roland Gaucher (Secker and Warbug, 1968)

The age of Terrorism by Walter Laqueur (Weidenfeld and Nicolson, 1987)

Terrorism and the liberal state (2nd ed.) by Paul Wilkinson (Macmillan, 1986)

The Assassins by Bernard Lewis, Oxford University press, April 1987

The day that shook the world by the BBC news team (BBC books, 2001)

J. Romains- in war there are no innocent victims

Albert Camus- The plague "The Greenhaven Press" ISBN#0-7377 0691-0-90000

About the Author

Jude Jacques was born in Port-au-Prince, Haiti. Growing up, he attended College Freres Gabriel, College Juvenat, and College Canado. His father, a colonel in the Haitian Army, and his mother, a businesswoman, sent him to live in the United States of America, a move that marked an exodus to save the family from persecution once Jean-Claude Duvalier, the country's former dictator, was exiled. In New York City, the author attended Erasmus Hall High School. He then enrolled in York College and later as an exchange student at the Sorbonne. Four years later, he earned a bachelor degree in French literature and education. Later, he received a master's degree from Hofstra University and a P.D from St. John's University. Dr. Jacques has taught college and secondary level education for many years, and he is currently teaching French and ESL (English as a second language) at the prestigious Hempstead High School in Nassau, Long Island.